The Tour

Dedication

Gordon (Tom) Raybould (15th June 1935 – 20th July 2018)

I first met Tom in the old Silver Ring at Newbury racecourse in the mid 1970's. We soon became good friends. Before too long we were heading off to the races far and wide, going horse racing at York, the Prix de l'Arc de Triomphe at Longchamp racecourse in Paris, Chantilly, the Dubai World Cup, Hong Kong and Australia.

Tom was a great fan of Steve Cauthen, the American jockey who came to race in the UK in 1979 and was very successful in the 80's. I used to say that Tom would have backed a rocking horse if Steve was riding it!

I remember on one occasion at Newbury racecourse when Tom and I had backed different horses in one race. I kept going on that I had a sneaking hunch for a second horse at long odds which the trainer of my horse had running in the same race.

"Go on" Tom said to me, "Put £1 on for me", which I did together with my £1. We were the only two punters in the Grandstand cheering home that 20/1 winner!

On another occasion, this time at York, once again we had backed different horses in the same race. We were both cheering them on as they fought out the finish and flashed past the winning post together. After 20 minutes or so we got the perfect result – a dead heat.

Going racing is not the same now without you mate.

FOREWORD

I first became interested in horse racing when I was about 14 years old. I used to watch the racing on ITV and BBC and started to pick horses out from the daily paper for fun and see how they got on.

Initially I used to assess horses form based on their past form figures with moderate success. However, I soon realised that a horse which came second could have been beaten a long way by the winner and a horse that finished third in another race might only have been beaten by two short heads.

Being quite tall for my age when I got to around 16½ I could pass for 18 so I started to frequent the local betting shop. I would make my selections and decide my staking plan using the information I could glean from the racing pages of The Sun newspaper then pop down to the local bookies to put my bets on for the afternoon, totalling the grand sum of 50p!

I would then watch the afternoon's racing and, more often than not, have to go back to the bookies later to collect my winnings.

I would generally restrict my bets to the televised racing. In those days there were no televisions in betting shops. Non televised races were only covered by the Extel commentary.

Being a red-blooded heterosexual young man, I developed an interest in a horse called Knockers. I backed it successfully on several occasions. On one occasion though I noticed that Knockers was running in a non-televised race, the 4:00 at Newbury. I decided to risk my whole 50p stake that day by putting it 'on the nose' on Knockers.

The afternoon's televised racing came and went and I awaited the late racing results. The result came 4:00 Newbury 1st Knockers 7/1! A relative fortune for a young teenager £4 return (less 10% tax in those days).

I was hooked

A couple of schoolfriends of mine, Keith and Cliff, were also interested in horse racing and we started to go racing, usually in the silver ring at local racecourses, usually Kempton Park and Windsor. In 1978 we became annual members at the newly re-opened Sandown Park after its modernisation. Later on, we started heading up and down the country going racing by train using ½ price Persil vouchers. Before long I realised that we had visited nearly half of the racecourses in the country. I then decided to visit them all and in 1988 I completed the last one at Catterick.

I retired from my day job as a Systems Librarian at British Airways at the age of 60 in 2015 so had much more free time available to go horse racing. I decided that I would like to revisit all of the UK racecourses while I was still young enough, healthy enough and had the stamina to do so. I had not been to some for nearly 40 years. A couple had closed (Folkestone and Stockton) and two new ones have opened (Chelmsford City and Ffos Las).

I decided to set myself the target of visiting all 61 racecourses on the UK mainland in a single calendar year.

I was an annual member of several racecourses (Ascot, Newbury, Sandown Park and York) and joined Fontwell Park as an annual member in 2017. So, with various reciprocal race days and admission to all of the 16 racecourses in the Arena Leisure Group using my Fontwell badge and going racing mostly on day trips (to avoid overnight hotel stays) I would be able to keep costs down to a manageable level.

When the 2017 Racing fixture list was published, I set about planning my racecourse tour.

2017 Racecourse Tour

Planned Schedule

Day	Date	Racecourse	Day	Date	Racecourse	Day	Date	Racecourse
Mon	02 Jan	Plumpton	Fri	31 Mar	Wetherby	Mon	22 May	Carlisle
Wed	04 Jan	Hereford	Sat	01 Apr	Stratford-On-Avon	Tue	23 May	Brighton
Thu	05 Jan	Lingfield Park	Tue	04 Apr	Newton Abbot	Sun	28 May	Uttoxeter
Sat	07 Jan	Sandown Park	Thu	06 Apr	Aintree	Mon	29 May	Chelmsford City
Wed	18 Jan	Newbury	Fri	07 Apr	Sedgefield	Wed	31 May	Beverley
Sat	21 Jan	Ascot	Sat	08 Apr	Chepstow	Sat	03 Jun	Hexham
Fri	10 Feb	Bangor-On-Dee	Mon	10 Apr	Kelso	Mon	05 Jun	Thirsk
Tue	28 Feb	Leicester	Wed	12 Apr	Catterick Bridge	Wed	07 Jun	Hamilton Park
Thu	02 Mar	Ludlow	Sat	15 Apr	Musselburgh	Tue	13 Jun	Yarmouth
Tue	07 Mar	Newcastle	Mon	17 Apr	Redcar	Wed	14 Jun	Worcester
Wed	08 Mar	Fontwell Park	Thu	20 Apr	Cheltenham	Mon	19 Jun	Windsor
Thu	09 Mar	Wincanton	Mon	24 Apr	Pontefract	Thu	22 Jun	Ripon
Tue	14 Mar	Southwell	Wed	26 Apr	Epsom Downs	Sun	02 Jul	Cartmel
Wed	15 Mar	Huntingdon	Thu	27 Apr	Perth	Sat	08 Jul	Haydock Park
Thu	16 Mar	Towcester	Mon	01 May	Bath	Tue	11 Jul	Wolverhampton
Fri	17 Mar	Fakenham	Tue	02 May	Nottingham	Thu	13 Jul	Doncaster
Sat	18 Mar	Kempton Park	Sat	06 May	Goodwood	Tue	25 Jul	Ffos Las
Mon	20 Mar	Taunton	Sun	07 May	Newmarket (Rowley)	Sat	05 Aug	Newmarket (July)
Tue	21 Mar	Exeter	Mon	08 May	Ayr	Mon	07 Aug	Salisbury
Wed	22 Mar	Warwick	Thu	11 May	Chester			
Mon	27 Mar	Market Rasen	Wed	17 May	York			

Monday 2nd January - Plumpton

The journey begins. My New Year resolution -to go horse racing at all 61 of the UK mainland racecourses in a single calendar year and raise £15,000 for 3 charities (the Injured Jockeys Fund, British Heart Foundation and Prostate Cancer UK) in the process.

I have been interested in horse racing since 1968 at the age of 14 when I used to watch it and the almost impossible to win 'ITV 7' on ITV.

On Bank Holiday Monday 27th May 1974 I went racing for the first time. The next day I went racing was the corresponding race meeting the following year. On 6th June 1980 I had visited all of the UK mainland racecourses. Today I begin my attempt to go racing at all of them again in 2017, except for Stockton and Folkestone which have since closed, plus Ffos Las and Chelmsford City (Great Leighs in its previous short-lived incarnation) which have both opened in the last few years.

Due to the ongoing rail strikes on Southern, there was the possibility of delays and cancellations so I decided to drive to Plumpton races today. I somehow managed to arrive at the racecourse around an hour before the first race at 12:50, driving along numerous B roads after I left the M23 a few miles south of Gatwick Airport. Plumpton racecourse is not well signposted until the Wivelsfield area, a few miles from the course.

Plumpton is a small village about 5 miles north-west of Lewes, which incidentally used to have a racecourse until it closed on Monday 14th September 1964. The parish also includes the larger village of Plumpton Green. Plumpton is best known for its racecourse and to a lesser extent, Plumpton College (formerly known as Plumpton Agricultural College). Plumpton is mentioned in the Domesday Book of 1086 as having a church and two mills, and is shown as 'Pluntune', meaning 'town or settlement where plum-trees grew'.

It was a lovely sunny day, and half of the hurdles were omitted in the opening race. My selection in the first race, Sporty Yankee was well in touch in midfield for most of the race, a 2 mile hurdle, until it faded and eventually finished a well beaten 5th by the time it reached the winning post. Laissez Dire, my pick in the 2nd race, a 2 mile steeplechase, fared even worse, falling fatally injured at the 9th obstacle.

I managed to get 2/1 winner in the 3rd race, No Comment, which stayed on well to beat the 13/8 favourite Minella Daddy by 2 lengths. My selection in race 4, Ding Ding was beaten 2 ¾ lengths into 3rd place.

Things were looking good for me with Sartorial Elegance in the big race of the day, the 3 ½ mile Sussex National, on what is Plumpton's best race day of the year. I had backed it at 13.5 (12.5/1) on Betfair and it was beginning to challenge and a close 5th when it unseated Paul O'Brien at the 17th fence.

Nil desperandum. Johns Luck did the business for me at 4/1 in the 6th race, a 2 ½ mile chase, driven out to win by a neck. Shimba Hills, the 9/4 favourite, rounded off the day for me by winning the 7th and final race of the day by half a length.

3 winners out of 7 and a profit on the day. Not a bad start!

The drive home was interesting to say the least. My car was parked in the centre of the course and I left via a different exit from the way I drove in. I drove through villages I had never heard of as the light faded into dark. Westmeston, Ditchling, Lindfield (not to be confused with Lingfield where I am planning to go racing on Thursday), Ardingley, Crawley Down and Turners Hill before I eventually found the M23.

Wednesday 4th January - Hereford

Another beautiful day. The 8am precautionary inspection was cancelled and racing goes ahead. Hereford racecourse recently reopened after being closed for 4 years. I decided to drive to the races today as God's Worst Railway (GWR) wanted an arm and a leg for a Day Return fare! A lovely drive through the English countryside passing near fantastically named villages such as Redmarley D'Abitot and Little Marcle.

Hereford is a cathedral city and the county town of Herefordshire. The name "Hereford" is said to come from the Anglo-Saxon "here", an army or formation of soldiers, and "ford", a place for crossing a river. If this is the origin it suggests that Hereford was a place where a body of armed men forded or crossed the river Wye. Nell Gwynne, actress and mistress of King Charles II is said to have been born in Hereford (although other towns and cities, notably Oxford also claim her as their own); Gwynne Street in Hereford is named after her.

I arrived at the racecourse 30 minutes before the first race and managed to back the winner - Late Shipment. I then saw a good friend of mine who I hadn't seen for years! "Hello you old bugger!" I said as I went to shake his hand. He looked at me quizzically. "I don't know you" he said. "My name is Stevens" he continued. "You are the spitting image of a friend of mine" I replied, "They say we all have a doppelgänger" I continued, before walking away. Later in the day I asked his permission to take his photo and I emailed it to my friend Tom Raybould who I had mistaken him for. He replied that it was him, only ten years ago!

Katy P could only manage a distant 3rd for me in the 2nd race. I took a chance with The Greenvet at 66/1 in the third race, which showed some promise for a short while before dropping back at the 7th and was well behind when it unseated Robert Dunne at the 9th fence. I had a few quid on Working Title, the 15/8 favourite in the 2:25, however it didn't get very far, falling at the 2nd obstacle.

At 5/4 favourite I decide not to back my fancy, Jameson in the 5th race. That proved to be a good decision as it was beaten 7 lengths into 3rd by Keeper Hill and Skipthecuddles.

Strong Pursuit was a very warm favourite at the prohibitive odds of 4/9 in race 6, so I decided to back Sandymount, the 11/4 2nd favourite to have an interest in the race. It finished 4th, beaten over 20 lengths. The interesting (at least to me!) part of the race was when the racecourse commentator announced that Katie Price's horse Bandon Bridge was going well. Had the former glamour model, previously known as Jordan taken up race riding? How could I have missed this change of career? The answer was simple. The Page 3 girl was not in fact riding. The horse was in fact trained by Katy (with a 'y') Price.

To round off the day I back Peruvien Bleu in the last race which finished last! Hey ho that's racing!

A sharp frost is predicted tonight so my planned day's jump racing tomorrow at Lingfield Park hangs in the balance.

Thursday 5th January - Chelmsford City

As I feared, the turf jump meeting at Lingfield Park was abandoned due to a heavy overnight frost. I quickly came up with Plan B and decided to go racing at Chelmsford City today. This was a new racecourse for me. I never managed to go racing there in its previous incarnation as Great Leighs racecourse.

A few random facts about Chelmsford. A roman fort was built in AD60, and a civilian town grew up around it. The town was given the name of Caesaromagus (the market place of Caesar). Chelmsford was significantly involved in the Peasants' Revolt of 1381, and Richard II moved on to the town after quelling the rebellion in London. During World War II Chelmsford, an important centre of light engineering war production, was attacked from the air on several occasions, both by aircraft of the Luftwaffe and by missile. The worst single loss of life took place on Tuesday 19th December 1944, when the 367th Vergeltungswaffe 2 or V2 rocket to hit England fell on a residential street near the Hoffman's ball bearing factory and not far from the Marconi Wireless Telegraph Company factory in New Street which may have been the real target. 39 people were killed and 138 injured, 47 seriously.

Although I understand that the racing surface is good, Chelmsford City racecourse must be the worst racecourse in the world for visibility. The grandstand is situated in the middle of the course making it impossible to view all but the last couple of furlongs of most races except on the big screen. The racecourse is also the worst signposted I have ever seen. There are no signs for Chelmsford Park racecourse. I happened to know that it is situated on the site of what used to be Essex County Showground so followed signs to that instead, hoping that the floodlights I could see were at the racecourse and not Chelmsford City Football Club . Fortunately I was correct!

Pendo finished 3rd for me in the first race. Western Prince managed only 5th in the second race. I was on the phone to my girlfriend so missed the chance to back Distant Past which finished a distant 5th in the third race. Secret Bird was too short for me to back at odds of 5/6 in the 7:15 so I did not have a bet in the race. It came third.

I decided to oppose Draw Swords, the even money favourite in the 7:45 and backed Speedo Boy instead getting 7/1 on it, beating the SP of 6/1. Amazingly it won, beating Draw Swords by ½ a length in a driving finish.

I rounded the evening off backing Shypen in the last race, which finished 8th of the 9 runners.

So that was my first and probably my last visit to Chelmsford City racecourse. I thought that Les Landes racecourse in Jersey was bad, but at least you can see the races from its tiny grandstand.

The weather is due to improve so hopefully my next planned racecourse visit, to Sandown Park for Tolworth Hurdle day on Saturday will be OK.

Saturday 7th January - Sandown Park

Day 4. Arrived at the racecourse to find that The Hogshead brewery stand had been replaced by Sandown Craft Ales. No Punter ale for me then! Decided to have a cup of tea instead.

Today I went racing with a good friend of mine Keith, who I went to school with and have been going horse racing with since 1974.

Before racing commenced, I received a phone call from Australia from Savita, another good friend. We chatted for 15 minutes and she agreed to come to the opening day of Royal Ascot this year with my girlfriend Christine and me.

A few random facts about Sandown Park racecourse. It was one of the first racecourses to charge everyone for admission. It opened in 1875 and everyone had to pay at least half a crown (12.5p). The first meeting took place on Thursday 22nd April and included the Grand National Hunt Chase, which is now staged at the Cheltenham festival. The Grand International Steeplechase took place on the Saturday and was worth £2,130 to the winner, more than the Grand National and was the largest prize for a steeplechase that season. Sandown Park also became the first course in England to have a Members enclosure. Between 1940 and 1945 Sandown Park was requisitioned by the War Department for World War II.

Coeur De Lion was unbackable at 1/3 favourite in the first race so I decided to keep my money in my pocket. Keith backed Don Bersy at 8/1, beating the SP of 7/1 and beating the odds on favourite by a comfortable 1 ½ lengths. After the race I met another friend of mine Denis. I asked him if he had backed the first winner. He replied that he would have done if he had arrived at the racecourse in time, adding "I hope it's not the only winner I would have had!".

Keith and I both backed Lifeboat Mona in the 12:50 and were rewarded as the joint favourite obliged, staying on well to beat Midnight Jazz by a comfortable 3 lengths. We both backed Atirelarigo in the 3rd race. It didn't get very far, falling at the 2nd fence when in last place.

I backed Garde La Victoire in the 4th race, getting 2/1 about the 6/4 favourite, which beat Bold Henry, the winner of the corresponding race last year by 2 lengths.

I chose not to have a bet in race 5, as the horse I fancied, Finian's Oscar was too short a price in my opinion. It was backed in from 6/4 to 11/10 justifying favouritism and winning with consummate ease by 5 lengths. One to keep an eye on for the Cheltenham Festival in March I think!

Rocky Creek, my selection in the 3:00 managed to beat only one home, .after racing prominently early in the race.

Keith and I both backed Robinshill in the last race at double digit odds. It led and was going well into the straight and looking like the winner until just after the last flight, before being headed about 60 yards before the line and going down by ¾ of a length.

That's it for me until Wednesday week at Newbury, weather permitting. Christine and I are flying to Dubai tonight and going on an Arabian Cruise next week.

Harold Wilson is credited with the saying "A week is a long time in politics". The same is obviously true in horse racing. I arrived home from my Arabian Cruise on Monday this week to the shocking news that Jockey Club Racecourses are planning to close Kempton Park racecourse for housing development and build an all-weather track at Newmarket! Hopefully neither will come to fruition.

This morning's news was unexpected but less shocking. After a colder than anticipated night Newbury called a precautionary inspection for 9:30 this morning. A second inspection was held at 11am and a 3rd one at 12:00, after which today's racecard was finally given the go-ahead. It was a clear day yesterday so you didn't need to be an Einstein to realise it was going to be a cold night yet the frost covers were only deployed on the far side of the racecourse. The temperature fell to -4C overnight. Fortunately, the frost came out of the ground in time for racing to take place.

Racing first took place at its current location at Newbury on 26/27 September 1905. At the time the Jockey Club had strict rules for new racecourses. John Porter, the Kingsclere trainer had his proposal for Newbury racecourse rejected several times before a chance meeting with King Edward II brought about a further application, which with the King's support was approved by the Jockey Club. During the First World War Newbury Racecourse was used as a prisoner-of-war camp for German prisoners.

On 12th February 2011 an unusual incident took place at the racecourse. Two horses collapsed and died in the paddock while parading for the first race. Two other horses also appeared to be affected. The first race went ahead, starting about 20 minutes late, but the rest of the card was abandoned. It later transpired that there had been leakage from an electrical cable running under the parade ring. Both the horses were examined post mortem and sudden cardiac arrest, consistent with accidental electrocution was established as the cause of death.

Due to the uncertainty over whether racing was going to take place today or not I delayed travelling until the 'all clear' was given. I missed the first race, which I was not going to have a bet in anyway as Final Choice, the 2/9 favourite seemed the obvious choice and was unbackable at the price. It led until 3 furlongs out before weakening badly and finishing last of the 4 runners, beaten 46 lengths!

Nicky Henderson's runner, Beyond Conceit, which had been off the track for nearly 3 ½ years (1,267 days to be precise) since finishing a close 4th at Glorious Goodwood in July 2013, emerged as the easy winner of the 2nd race, triumphing by 10 lengths at 3/1. My selection, Royal Hall finished 5th.

I met Maurice, a friend of mine just before the off of the 3rd race. He advised me that my selection, Red Devil Star (which was drifting like a barge in the betting), had never won on soft ground. Red Devil Star was in touch and going OK when he was badly hampered when Britanio Bello fell at the 7th fence giving Michael Nolan no chance of staying aboard, and unseating him. Maurice had backed both Theatre Flame (the 10/1 winner) and Champagne At Tara (2/1). "I've got the forecast here", he said to me between the last two fences, "All they have to do is stand up". Unfortunately for him though, although they did both successfully negotiate the final obstacle, Max Ward, the 7/4 favourite came with a good late run to split them in the run to the line after the last.

During the afternoon I also met my racing friend Keith and two of his friends Jen & Pete from Arrochar (near Loch Lomond) in Scotland. Keith backed Brandon Hill, the 11/2 winner of the 4th race. My selection Monbeg Gold raced prominently for most of the race before eventually fading into 5th.

Theatre Territory was the 4/9 hot favourite in the 5th race and was going like the winner when falling 2 out. Fortunately I made the wise decision not to have a bet in the race. Pete however made an even wiser decision, by backing Midnight Glory, the 25/1 winner!

I rounded off the day by backing Perfect Harmony at 15/2 which got up to win the bumper in the dying strides.

God's Worst Railway (GWR) lived up to their nickname as the driver of the 16:00 train from Newbury Racecourse failed to stop at the racecourse station!

Next stop on my racecourse tour is Ascot on Saturday. Weather permitting of course!

Saturday 21st January - Lingfield Park

Lingfield Park racecourse was opened in 1890 by the Prince of Wales (later Edward VII), who also agreed to let Lingfield incorporate the Prince of Wales feathers into its official logo. The course originally held jumps racing only, but in 1894 the Jockey Club granted permission for flat racing to be held. Racing has been held continuously since, the only exception being during World War II when the War Office requisitioned the course. The racecourse is featured in the 1954 film Rainbow Jacket.

Racing at Ascot today was abandoned due to frost following a 6:30am inspection this morning. I therefore decided to go racing at Lingfield today. I arrived just before the first race. It was a beautiful winter day, not a cloud in the sky and bright sunshine.

I had a few quid on Byres Road. In an exciting finish Franco's Secret a 7/1 shot got up in the dying strides to deny Chevalier, the 7/4 favourite. Byres Road chased the leader early on but weakened inside the final furlong, finishing 5th at the line. After the first race I saw a friend of mine, Mac, who I usually see at Ascot races. "I see you're slumming it as well today!" he said. I then went to try to obtain a racecard. They were sold out. "It's the crowd from Ascot that are the problem", the guy said to me. "I know", I said, "I'm one of them!" Special thanks to Glynne and Pat, a couple from Uttoxeter who were originally planning to go racing at Ascot today and Fontwell Park tomorrow, for taking my racecourse photo today holding one of their racecards!

I backed Indian Dandy, the 13/8 favourite in the second race in a double with Al Yarmouk, the favourite in race 6. Indian Dandy proceeded to unship Luke Morris and ran about until caught. He was then withdrawn, and all bets made prior to his withdrawal were subject to a 35p in the £ Rule 4 deduction. My friend Mac backed Mailshot at 6/4 prior to the withdrawal of Indian Dandy, reducing its price to just under evens (39/40 to be precise), after the Rule 4 deduction. In the reformed market Mailshot went off the 4/9 favourite and ran on well to win the race readily by 2 ½ lengths.

After the race I noticed a memorial to Davy Jones of The Monkees, who used to be a stable lad and won a race at Lingfield before he came to fame. "You don't know who The Monkees are, do you?" a passer-by commented to me. "I am afraid I am that old!" I responded.

My selection Seven Clans at Even money favourite was too short for me to contemplate backing in the third race which was fortunate, as he got chinned on the line by Etaad, which drifted from 13/2 to 14/1, but came with a wet sail to win by a short head in the final stride.

Rock Steady carried my hopes in the fourth event, the most valuable race on the card, but was beaten into 2nd place by Pinzolo the 5/2 favourite in a sustained duel in the final furlong, creating a new course record for 2 1/.2 miles in a time of 2 min 26.99 seconds, beating the record by 0.10 secs.

Green Or Black could only manage fifth place for me behind Enmeshing in the 3:10. Things were beginning to look bleak for my prospects with only two races remaining!

In the sixth race, Al Yarmouk the 11/8 favourite carried my hopes in what was now a single bet (due to Indian Dandy's antics before the 1:25). He eventually lost out to Revolutionary War the 7/4 second favourite in a dogfight all the way up the straight, prevailing by a head in the last few strides.

In the getting out stakes, Bridge Builder was my final hope of the day of backing a winner. Amazingly he did the business for me, keeping on well to win by a comfortable length and three quarters.

I am whisking my girlfriend off for another holiday to the sunshine of South Africa this weekend which will include horse racing at Kenilworth and Turffontein in addition to a week in Cape Town, a drive along the Garden Route and a 5 day safari in Kruger National Park. After which I am hoping to go racing at Bangor-on-Dee the day after we return to Blighty.

Friday 10th February - Bangor-on Dee

Chrissie and I returned from South Africa yesterday morning. We went racing at Kenilworth and Turffontein as planned. We also had an 'interesting' stay (to say the least!) at the Tremisana Game Lodge in the Balule Nature Reserve at Kruger. If you fancy a good laugh, I suggest you read the 'Poor' and 'Terrible' reviews for both Tremisana and Marc's Treehouse Lodge in TripAdvisor!

Racing first took place at Bangor-on-Dee racecourse in February 1859 and has since taken place regularly except during the First and Second World Wars. Since 2006 Bangor has also hosted amateur Point-to-Point races run by local hunts. The Point-to-Point course is on the inside of the main track. Bangor racecourse is unusual insofar as it does not have a grandstand.

Back to today's action. Bangor-on-Dee passed an early morning inspection so off I headed on a 178 mile drive (according to Google Maps), via some wonderfully named villages, e.g. Cockshutt and Preston Gubbals. Today was my third visit to Bangor-on-Dee races. The last one was 8,476 days ago on 11th September 1993. Bangor is an unusual racecourse in several respects. It has a separate point-to-point track in the centre. It also does not have a grandstand with racegoers watching the action from a grass bank open to the elements from the Paddock enclosure. The winning post is also unusual insofar as it is viewed 'head on' so the video screen is essential to watch in a tight finish.

I arrived 30 minutes before the first race. I was contemplating having a double on Over To Sam, the 4/6 favourite in the opener with Antartica De Thaix, which was forecast to be the 4/7 favourite in the second race. In the end I decided that the potential reward did not justify the financial risk so I decided not to have a bet in race 1. That proved to be a wise decision as Over To Sam, which raced prominently until two flights from home eventually finished third, behind Testify the 11/2 winner.

Antartica De Thaix. The Paul Nicholls runner, started at the generous odds of Even Money favourite in the second race so I decided it was worth a bet. Sainte Ladylime and Antartica De Thaix drew well clear of the rest of the field. Antartica De Thaix had just about got the measure of Sainte Ladylime at the second last fence at which the latter made a bad mistake and crumpled on landing, leaving Sean Bowen's mount to record a bloodless 49 lengths victory over Lochnell.

Dashing Oscar started the 8/15 favourite in the third race. My selection, Cosmos Des Obeaux drifted from 5/2 to 9/2 in the betting. Neither of them won, the prize instead being claimed by Dashing Oscar's half-brother Cousin Oscar at 100/30.

Themanfrom Minella, my fancy in the fourth race (a 3 mile 5 furlongs marathon), never got into the race and was eventually pulled up, with Barton Gift winning by a comfortable five lengths from Lord Heathfield.

Surprise vendor, which carried the additional burden of the weight of my money, led for most of the fifth race before fading into seventh at the post. Victory went to Beggar's Wishes at 15/2.

Samson's Reach recorded a shock 100/1 win in the bumper, triumphing over Atlantic Grey by 1 ¾ lengths. Clondaw Rigger, my fancy in the race finished fifth.

My selection in the Hunter Chase, Big Fella Thanks was a non-runner and as I didn't fancy any of the remaining runners, I decided to head off home early while it was still light.

Chrissie and I are heading off to the Isles of Scilly for ten days next week. My next planned stop on my racecourse tour is Leicester on Tuesday 28th February although I may go to Kempton Park on Saturday 25th and Fontwell Park on Sunday 26th February (all weather dependent of course).

Saturday 25th February - Kempton Park

I arrived home from the Isles of Scilly yesterday evening so off I go to Kempton Park today on Leg 8 of my UK Racecourse Tour!

Kempton Park racecourse was the idea of the 19th Century businessman S.H. Hyde, who was enjoying a carriage drive in the country when he came across Kempton Manor and Park for sale. Hyde leased the grounds in 1872 and six years later in July 1878 Kempton opened as a racecourse.

Kempton Park racecourse was redeveloped in 2005/2006, since when all flat racing at the course has been run on the new all-weather Polytrack, which has floodlighting to enable racing to take place in all but the most severe bad weather.

In January 2017 the Jockey Club announced the closure of Kempton Park by 2021, following the local authority's 'Call for Sites' to address unmet housing needs. The plan includes moving some of the most important jump races such as the King George VI Chase and the Christmas Hurdle to Sandown Park, with the other jumps fixtures spread around other Jockey Club owned racecourses and the all-weather track to be replaced by a new artificial track to be built at Newmarket. Thankfully, at the time of writing, there has been no further movement on this proposal, and hopefully it will not take place.

Picked up my racing mate Keith this morning and drove to Kempton. Enjoyed a pint of real ale before Race 1.

Had a few quid on Coastal Tiep, one of Paul Nicholls runners in the first race. It was held up for most of the race and was close up and looked promising approaching the last obstacle, pressed the winner after the last flight but was always held and finished 1 ¼ lengths behind River Frost the 5/1 favourite.

The favourites in the second and third races, Charli Parcs and Frodon both looked like good things so Keith and I decided not to bet in races 2 and 3. We did however decide in the space of the next 30 minutes to go racing in Ireland for the Punchestown Winter Festival and booked our flights!

Charli Parcs, the 8/15 favourite, was held up for most of the second race and appeared to be struggling before he crumpled on landing at the second last. Master Blueyes claiming the prize at 13/2.

Frodon fared better in the third race, justifying his starting price of 8/11, staying on well to beat Nicky Henderson's Present Gold by a comfortable 2 lengths.

I was torn between three horses in the fourth race, Elgin, Peter The Mayo Man and River Wylde. I plumped for Elgin, which had finished well, behind top prospect Neon Wolf at Haydock Park in a Grade 2 event last time out, having won his previous two hurdle races. Elgin tracked River Wylde and Peter The Mayo Man for most of the race and had every chance before making a mistake at the last which may have cost him the race. River Wylde won the race. At least I can claim the bragging rights of having selected the first three home, albeit not in the correct order, as Peter The Mayo Man filled the frame. Second again!

Cocktails at Dawn and Double Shuffle (my selection) led and were well clear of the rest of the field for most of the fifth race. When Cocktails at Dawn fell at the eighth the race looked at my mercy. However Pilgrims Bay (which I backed when it won at Sandown Park at 9/1 last December) was still on the bridle and led at the last, winning at the generous odds of 25/1 today! Second yet again!

My fancy in the sixth, Sir Note, drifted alarmingly in the betting from 7/2 to 7/1. Fortunately the horse did not realise that he was unfancied in the market, led for most of the race and was left with an easy task to beat Full Shift when Gores Island suffered a crashing fall at the last.

A winner at last!

Keith and I decided to leave before the bumper, which looked like a formality for Champ, Nicky Henderson's 4/6 favourite, which actually finished a readily held second behind Irish Prophecy.

Next stop Fontwell Park tomorrow.

Sunday 26th February - Fontwell Park

Leg 9. Two hour drive to Fontwell Park, passing by another magnificently named village. Burpham Merrow!

Fontwell Park racecourse was founded by Alfred Day who trained racehorses at The Hermitage, by the Chichester to Arundel Road from 1887. By 1924 he had purchased enough land to open a racecourse at Fontwell. The hurdles track was a normal shape, but the steeplechase course was laid out in a figure of eight to use the space on the site. The first meeting took place on 21st May 1924.

Fontwell Park is the racecourse where Queen Elizabeth II, then Princess Elizabeth, had her first winner as an owner when Monaveen won the Chichester Handicap Chase in October 1949.

Met my friend Maurice by chance at the races today, who was talking with Ron Atkins, who was a jockey in the 1970's.

As chance would have it Maurice is planning to go racing at Towcester on Thursday 16th March and Aintree on the opening day of the Grand National meeting on Thursday 6th April, so we arranged to meet up on both of these dates, as I already have them planned in as part of my racecourse tour.

My selection in the first race today, Kilcrea Vale opened at 4/5 and touched 8/11 before going out to 10/11 favourite. I had decided I was only going to back it if I could get Even money so I put in a request for that price on my Betfair account. Fortunately it was matched just before the off, as Kilcrea Vale disputed the lead for most of the race and won by 2 lengths. As De Mee led for most of the race and looked the likely winner until it ran out of petrol approaching the last fence. In fact Maurice, who had backed As De Mee, commented to me as they turned for home "I'd rather be on mine than yours!". Famous last words!

My planned selection in the 2:30, Johns Luck, which won for me at Plumpton on 2nd January was a non-runner, so I plumped for King Of Glory instead. He tracked the leaders for most of the race but after hitting the 10th weakened 2 out, and eventually finishing 40 lengths behind Wizards Bridge the 2/1 favourite, which won the race by a comfortable 4 lengths from The Italian Yob.

Different Gravey carried my hopes (and money) in the principal race of the day, the £80,000 National Spirit Hurdle, the most valuable race staged at Fontwell Park in the year. Unfortunately Different Gravey was never travelling and looked a forlorn hope a circuit before the finish. Camping Ground led throughout and stayed on strongly to beat Le Rocher by a comfortable 29 lengths at the rewarding odds of 9/1!

I backed the Paul Nicholls runner, Peak To Peak in the 3:30, however despite tracking the leaders for most of the race it could finish only fifth behind Crystal Lad, which raced prominently throughout and was well in command at the business end of the race beating Sir Antony Browne the 2/1 favourite by an easy 7 lengths.

As the Paul Nicholls runners were not faring well today, I decided to take on Mon Parrain, the 1/3 favourite in the Hunter Chase, backing Current Exchange, the 5/1 second favourite instead. However Mon Parrain justified his prohibitive odds, beating my selection easily by 26 lengths.

Ding Ding was saddled with my selection in the sixth race. Ding Ding was in touch until three flights from the finish, before weakening into fifth place nearly 40 lengths behind Seas Of Green, the easy 12/1 winner.

As I am not a fan of 'bumpers' (as National Hunt Flat races are colloquially known), I left before the last. Puppet Warrior the 5/6 Nick Gifford trained favourite, finished 2nd behind Larry, the Gary Moore trained 6/1 winner.

Next stop Leicester on Tuesday.

Tuesday 28th February - Leicester

Leicester is one of the oldest cities in England with a history dating back at least two millennia. The native Iron Age settlement encountered by the Romans at the site seems to have developed in the 2nd or 1st centuries BC.

At the end of the War of the Roses, King Richard III was buried in Leicester's Greyfriars Church, a Franciscan Friary which was demolished in 1538. There was a legend that his corpse had been cast into the river, while some historians argued that his tomb and remains were destroyed during the dissolution of the monasteries under Henry VIII. However in September 2012, an archaeological investigation of the car park revealed a skeleton, which DNA testing, together with the shape of the spine. later concluded that the skeleton was that of Richard III. In 2015 Richard III was reburied in pride of place near the high altar in Leicester Cathedral.

Leicester racecourse was the scene of the infamous Flockton Grey ringer case. Flockton Grey was entered into a race for two year olds on 29th March 1982. As a debutant from an unsuccessful yard (his trainer had failed to train a winner in two years), the horse was priced at 10/1. The perpetrators of the scam saw an opportunity to make a quick profit and backed the horse with £20,000, spreading the money around several different betting shops to avoided detection. They then arranged for a three year old horse, Good Hand to run in place of Flockton Grey.

Meeting his younger opponents at level weights, he had a huge advantage and unsurprisingly romped home, winning by 20 lengths. The margin of victory caused immediate suspicion and bookmakers refused to pay out. Once the deceit was uncovered one of the perpetrators was charged with conspiracy to defraud, and in June 1984 he was convicted, fined £20,000 with £125,000 costs and given a 9 month suspended jail sentence. Together with the other perpetrator he was also "warned off" racecourses for an unprecedented 25 years. The jockey, Kevin Darley was exonerated of any knowledge of the switch, and it was noted that a rider with inside knowledge could easily have held his horse back, minimising the winning margin to prevent any suspicion.

Two hour drive to Leicester today. I have only been racing here on two previous occasions, the latest of which was over 36 years ago (13,615 days ago to be precise), on 20th November 1979!

An unusual card today as all of the races were chases - no hurdle races or a bumper.

I intended to back Brice Canyon in the first race on Betfair at approximately 13/2. However I made a mistake and laid it instead at the same price! To make matters worse Brice Canyon contracted in the market ending up at 4/1. Portents not looking good as it was obviously well fancied! Fortunately however after leading for most of the race it was overtaken by both Ardmayle, the 9/2 winner and Gustav approaching the last so the bet was landed, albeit accidentally!

The 2:40 race turned into a match as the two outsiders were withdrawn. I decided not to have a bet as Belami Des Pictons, the unbackable 1/4 favourite looked a good thing on paper. Zeroshadesofgrey raced alongside Belami Des Pictons for most of the race and looked a potential danger entering the straight, however the favourite stretched clear, eventually prevailing by an easy 33 lengths.

As an aside I noticed that the food and drink at Leicester are very reasonably priced, with a cup of tea or coffee retailing at a very modest £1.20 and a bacon or sausage bap at £3.50.

I watched the second race on the TV and noticed that the SIS coverage was approximately 5 seconds behind the live action. Betfair customers beware!

I backed the Paul Nicholls trained favourite Rebel Rebellion in the principal race of the day, the Leicestershire Open Hunters Chase. It was held up in touch for most of the race before making a mistake at the thirteenth and weakening , eventually finishing in sixth place, 57½ lengths behind the 3/1 winner Galway Jack, which made all, beating Toby Lerone by 14 lengths.

Powerful Symbol could only manage a well beaten second for me in the 3:40, beaten 10 lengths by Sunny Ledgend.

Miss Oscarrose looked like she was in with a winning chance in the 4:10 until it made a dreadful blunder at the last, handing a 10 lengths victory to Midnight Mustang in the process.

I thought I might have been in with a chance on Supreme Danehill in the last when it was left in the lead at the ninth when The Highlander, the 8/11 favourite unshipped his rider. However Supreme Danehill weakened, eventually finishing 55 lengths behind Kristian Gray, the 10/1 winner.

Better luck at Ludlow on Thursday maybe?

Thursday 2nd March - Ludlow

The market town of Ludlow is situated in Shropshire and has a population of approximately 11,000. The place name Lodelowe was in use before 1138 and comes from the Old English hlud-hlaew. At the time this section of the River Teme contained rapids, so the hlud of Ludlow came from "the loud waters", whilst hlaew meant "hill" or tumulus. So the name Ludlow describes a place on the hill by the loud waters. The town was described by Sir John Betjeman as "probably the loveliest town in England".

Ludlow racecourse is crossed at three points by the B4365 and traffic is stopped when the course is in use. The racecourse is located between the small villages of Bromfield and Stanton Lacy, just off the A49, at a place long known as the Old Field.

It is nearly 40 years since my one and only previous visit to Ludlow races with my racing mate Keith on 12th May 1977. 14,539 days in fact! Memorable because we both selected Honey Blue which won for us at the handsome odds of 14/1.

147 miles and a 2 ½ hour drive to Ludlow today. Bright sunny day today, the 2nd day of meteorological spring. Saw some more signposts to more magnificently named villages, Richards Castle and Much Wenlock!

Ludlow is an unusual racecourse in a few respects. The saddling boxes, parade ring and winners enclosure are located in the centre of the course, similar to Chester. The chase course is also much tighter than the hurdles course, the two tracks are separate on the back stretch. Ludlow also has a water jump immediately in front of the stands, similar to Newbury.

My selection in the first race, Coopers Square opened at 9/1 and drifted out to 16/1. He raced reluctantly and was quickly tailed off, eventually pulling up 3 flights from home, Billy Hicks claiming the prize holding the persistent challenge of Be My Sea the 11/8 favourite, by 2 1/4 lengths at the line.

I opposed Kap Jazz, the 10/11 favourite , backing Colin's Brother instead, which gave me a glimmer of hope when he tried to get into contention at the 14th fence, where he made a mistake, eventually finishing last of the 3 finishers, beaten 26 lengths by Kap Jazz.

My fortunes did not improve in the 3:25, where Aliandy, the 2/1 favourite could only manage a remote last of the four finishers, beaten over 40 lengths by Seymour Star, the 8/1 winner.

Dusky Lark carried the additional burden of being my selection in the big race of the day, the £20,000 Fobra Gold Cup. He led initially, made mistakes at both the 13th and 14th fences, and was still vying for the lead 3 out, before fading and finishing 4th of the six finishers, behind Marcilhac the 100/30 winner, beaten just over 10 lengths, my closest finisher of the day!

My selection in the 4:35, Two Swallows was poor value opening at 6/4 hardening to 11/10 favourite. I therefore decided to leave the racecourse after the 4:00 as I had a long drive home, which took 3 ½ hours. Two Swallows did not justify its short odds, finishing 18 lengths behind Miss Tongabezi, the 6/1 winner.

I am going racing tomorrow and Saturday at Newbury before resuming my racecourse tour at Newcastle on Tuesday and Wincanton on Thursday next week.

Tuesday 7th March - Newcastle

Today is my eighth visit to Newcastle races, and my first since the turf on the Flat course was replaced with an all-weather Tapeta surface in 2016. My last visit here was on 14th April 2012. Today was in fact only my second day's National Hunt racing at Newcastle. My only previous day's jump racing at here was just over 29 years ago on Fighting Fifth Day in 1988!

I nearly didn't make it to Newcastle today. Due to a signalling problem on the Central Line I made it to Kings Cross with only 3 minutes to spare before the 09:30 train for which I had an Advance Purchase ticket. The cheapest fare on subsequent trains, a 'Super Off-Peak Single' including my 34% Senior Railcard discount, would have cost £86.95. Not very 'Super' in my book!

A few historical facts about Newcastle. The city developed around the Roman settlement Pons Aelius, founded in the 2nd Century AD. The population of Pons Aelius then is estimated at 2,000. Conflicts with the Danes in 876 left the settlements along the River Tyne in ruins. Because of its strategic position, Robert Curthouse, son of William the Conqueror, erected a wooden castle in 1080. The town was henceforth known as Novum Castellium or New Castle.

During World War II the city and surrounding area were a target for air raids as heavy industry was involved in the production of ships and armaments. The raids caused 141 deaths and 587 injuries. A former French consul in Newcastle called Jacques Serre assisted the German war effort by describing important targets in the region to Admiral Raeder who was head of the German Navy.

Back to today's racing.

After I arrived at Newcastle Central railway station, I took the Metro to Regent Centre, outside which a courtesy coach was waiting to take punters the 4 mile trip to the racecourse.

It was a fairly sunny day today at Gosforth Park, as Newcastle racecourse is otherwise known. The going was heavy and as a consequence there was only a total of 34 horses declared on the card.

The opener was a very poor race and looking at the form all of the horses seemed to have very little chance of winning! I backed Broadway Belle more in hope than anticipation and to have an interest in the race. It was held up for most of the race before being outpaced and plugging on, eventually finishing in third place, beaten 16 lengths behind Knocknamona the 11/8 favourite.

The 2:40 race, a chase over nearly 3 miles, only had 3 runners which turned into a match after the third fence which Mossies Well tipped up at. Whiskey Chaser the 3/1 outsider, led for most of the race, giving favourite backers, including myself a bit of a fright. Very little separated them for most of what turned out to be a good contest. Plus Jamais the 5/6 favourite, after some heavy driving, managed to get to Whiskey Chaser just before the post, winning by ½ a length in the end.

Manwell (not to be confused by Manuel the Spanish waiter in Fawlty Towers) carried my hopes in the third event, running keenly throughout the race and seeming to have every chance 2 out. Maybe his early exertions took their toll, as he was outpaced on the run-in, and finished in third place nearly 8 lengths behind Modulus the other 3/1 joint favourite, which kept on strongly to win by 2 ¼ lengths from Catching Shadows.

The second chase on the card only had four contestants. My selection, Two Smokin Barrels, the 11/10 favourite, tracked the leaders for most of the race, made a mistake at the 7th but soon recovered, before taking up the running and winning eased-down by five lengths from Asuncion, a 25/1 shot, the only other finisher in the race. The other two runners both having been pulled up.

The fifth race had a close finish, with Reverant Cust the 5/2 favourite staying on strongly to beat my selection Midnight Moss which kept on but was held by ¾ of a length in the end.

My fancy in the bumper, Sultans Pride was soon outpaced after racing too keenly and prominently early on before being outpaced and finishing second behind Niceandeasy which ran green before being driven out and winning nice and easy by 10 lengths.

Thursday 9th March - Wincanton

Prior to the Norman Conquest, Wincanton was frequently the scene of battles between the Britons, Danes and Saxons. During the reign of Edmund Ironside, the English, under his command, defeated the Danes, forcing them to leave England. In the Domesday Book the name of the town was spelled as "Wincaleton", thought to mean "Pleasant town on the Cale".

A good job I decided to bring my visit to Fontwell Park forward to Sunday 26th February as yesterday's race meeting there was abandoned due to waterlogging after heavy rain the night before.

Today is my ninth visit to Wincanton races. My last trip here was over 15 years ago! Bright sunny warm spring-like day in the sun with a slight breeze today. Going Heavy. A big crowd today as it is Bathwick Tyres Free Race Day. Free admission to all racegoers who ordered a ticket in advance, otherwise £14 on the gate today.

The steeplechase fences here are large, making it a good test of a chaser. Three fences in quick succession in the home straight make for exciting racing, and often change the complexion of races, resulting in a great many close finishes.

Flow With Eve was my pick in the opening 2 ½ mile hurdle. Unusually there were five greys in this race, four of which were almost white! Flow With Eve was held up towards the rear for most of the race and never really got into the race, beaten into 7th place 13 lengths behind Daytime Ahead, one of the almost white greys, the 14/1 winner.

Catchin Time carried my money in the next race. He tracked the leaders most of the way round but could not mount a serious challenge at the business end of the race, finally finishing in third place behind Unison the 11/8 favourite which won gamely by 1 ¼ lengths from Oscar Sunset.

I narrowed the third race down to Dawson City the 3/1 favourite and Flaming Charmer at 7/2. I backed the wrong one! Regal Flow was making a race of it with Dawson City with the pair well clear of the remainder of the field when he stumbled badly and unseated Sean Houlihan at the third last obstacle, leaving Dawson City only to jump the last two fences to win by 32 lengths from Top Wood, with Flaming Charmer a further 34 lengths behind in third place.

The favourites in the next two races were both long odds on so not decent betting propositions. Multiculture and Coole Cody duly both obliged at the prohibitive odds of 1/6 and 1/2 respectively.

Shanann Star was my last hope of the day as I had decided not to stay for the bumper. Shanann Star at least gave me a shout as she closed on the leader on the turn for home. However General Girling, a 50/1 shot stayed on well to beat Shanann Star by 6 lengths at the line.

Two days racing for me at Sandown Park tomorrow and Saturday before I resume my racecourse tour with a vengeance next week!

My only previous visit to Southwell races was a jump meeting on Bank Holiday Monday 29th August 1977, 14,442 days ago, three days after my 23rd Birthday! The course has changed significantly since then. It used to be a left-hand triangular course, rather like Ascot only going the other way around. It is now an oval course. The outer track is now an all-weather Fibresand surface.

During the English Civil War, King Charles I spent his last night as a free man in May 1646 in the Saracen's Head (then the King's Head), before surrendering to the Scottish Army. It is reputed that Oliver Cromwell also stayed in the King's Head.

The well-known Bramley cooking apple was first seeded in Southwell in 1809. The apple is now used across the cookery world and is renowned for its acidic taste and the fact that it cooks to a smooth puree. One of the local football clubs, Southwell City, is nicknamed "The Bramleys" in honour of the town's contribution to British cuisine. In March 2009, a stained glass window was installed in Southwell Minster, commemorating the Bramley apple's 200th anniversary.

I took the train from Kings Cross to Newark Northgate station today then walked about a mile to Newark Castle station, from which I caught the train to Rolleston station which is adjacent to the racecourse.

My selection in the opener Storm King was predicted to be the favourite in the morning paper. In the end Samtu started the 7/4 favourite, just ahead of Busy Street and Storm King in the market, which both went off at 2/1. The market told the story as that is how they finished with Samtu winning by 1 ¼ lengths with Storm King a further 1 ¼ lengths behind in third. Storm King travelled wide and tracked the winner, was close up three furlongs out before keeping on at the same pace.

Hungarian Rhapsody started the 5/6 favourite in the second race. I decided to take a chance on Darvie but also fancied Gnaad a bit. Needless to say Gnaad won the race at 11/4. Darvie chased the leading pair on the outer but could only manage third place at the line, four lengths behind Gnaad which kept on strongly beating Hungarian Rhapsody, which finished second, beaten by 1 ¾ lengths.

Borough Boy carried my hopes in the 2:25 race. He tracked the leaders for most of the race making reasonable headway two furlongs out and kept on under pressure. However Jacob's Pillow, the 9/4 favourite kept on better, beating Borough Boy by a length.

Escalating started favourite in the 3:05 carrying the additional burden of my wager. Escalating did not have the run of the race and lost place after a furlong, staying on at the business end of the race. However Crosse Fire, a 10/1 shot had already flown by then, and beat Escalating by 2 ¼ lengths.

Dose carried my hopes in the fifth race. She was in touch on the outer but lost place hallway through the one mile contest, staying on in the final furlong but only finishing in fifth place, 8 lengths behind Muqarred the 3/1 favourite, which kept on strongly, beating Pool House an 18/1 shot by 4 lengths.

I decided to saddle General Tufto as my selection in the 4:25. He was towards the rear and pushed along for a lot of the race before making headway two furlongs from home and staying on well under pressure, finishing second 1 ¼ lengths behind Hammer Gun the 6/4 favourite, which won at 100/1 in his previous outing at Southwell five days earlier!

Go On Gal completed a frustrating day for me in the last race, providing me with my fourth runner up of the day, keeping on well to chase Lady Turpin the 8/1 winner home, beaten by 2 ¼ lengths.

Wednesday 15th March - Huntingdon

Nearly ¼ of the way through already! Leg 15 of my Racecourse Tour today takes me to Huntingdon, the birthplace of Oliver Cromwell, the Lord Protector.

Huntingdon was founded by the Anglo-Saxons and Danes. It appears as Huntedun in the Domesday Book of 1086. The name means "The huntsman's hill". The George Hotel in Huntingdon, named after St George in 1574, was bought 25 years later by Henry Cromwell, grandfather of Oliver Cromwell. Charles I made the George Hotel his headquarters in 1645. The highwayman Dick Turpin is said to have been a visitor, when it was a coaching inn on the Great North Road.

I took the train from King's Cross to Huntingdon railway station today. Shortly afterwards a couple of courtesy people carriers arrived to take punters the three miles to the racecourse.

The Nicky Henderson trained Christmas In April carried my money in the opening event. He was held up in midfield for most of the race before making a mistake two out and keeping on one pace on the flat. So Celebre a 5/1 chance ran well throughout the race, running on well and drawing clear on the flat to win readily by four lengths from Burning Heat, the 50/1 runner-up.

I gave Miss Oscarrose which I backed at Leicester a couple of weeks ago and came so close to winning before making a dreadful hash at the last another chance. He was with the leaders until the second fence then lost its place and fell back to joint last place, made numerous subsequent errors and had no chance of winning with a circuit to race. He eventually managed to finish a very modest fourth, 31 lengths behind Benability, the 9/2 winner, which won by 6 lengths and was never seriously challenged.

I backed Meribel Mille, the 7/4 favourite in the 2 ½ mile Mares Handicap Hurdle. She was in touch before making a mistake and not having the clearest of runs three flights from home. After which she was well held and kept on one pace on the flat, finishing sixth of the nine runners, seven lengths behind Pretty Rose, the 14/1 winner.

Quill Art, my selection in the Ladies Riders' Handicap Hurdle started the 7/2 favourite. She was in touch in the middle of the pack until unseating her rider at the third flight.

Celtic Tune carried my money in the next race. He chased the leaders and had every chance three fences out and led at the bend before the second last. He went sharply left on the flat and was hard driven and pressed towards the finish and beaten close home by Rocknrollrambo, which triumphed by a neck.

The sixth race only had four runners and a long odds-on favourite, which looked like a good thing followed by a bumper, so I decided to head home after the 4:25 race.

Thursday 16th March - Towcester

Towcester lays claim to being one of the oldest continuously inhabited settlements in the country. It was the Roman town of Lactodorum, located on Watling Street, today's A5. Towcester features in Charles Dickens's novel The Pickwick Papers as one of Mr Pickwick's stopping places on his tour.

It is just over twenty years since my last visit to Towcester races. About an hour and a half drive today. Passed yet another magnificently named village en-route, Hinton-in-the-Hedges!

Three years ago Towcester racecourse opened a greyhound track opposite the main grandstand. It is tilted upwards on the far side and completely obscures the view of about half a mile of the racecourse. It is only possible to view most of the horse racing action on the far side of the racecourse by looking at the big screen. If I had wanted to watch horse racing on the television, I would have gone to a betting shop! Thankfully admission to Towcester racecourse is free!

My selection in the opening Conditional Jockeys' Handicap Hurdle was Daytime Ahead, the 15/8 favourite. He certainly did not justify favouritism! He never really got into the race and finished a very poor sixth, 33 lengths behind Goodnight Charlie the 9/2 winner.

General Girling gave me my first winner since Two Smokin Barrels at Newcastle on 7th March. General Girling was ridden confidently by my namesake, Mitchell Bastyan, leading at the twelfth obstacle and stayed on well to beat Gibbstown by a length at the post.

They say you can wait ages for a bus then two come together. Celestial Magic showed that the same can hold true for backing winners! Daniel Heskett held him up, made headway at the fourth flight, led before two out and was driven out to beat Authorized Too by a neck.

The next two races had long odds-on favourites and my fancy in the sixth race Midnight Request looked like it was likely to start as a short priced favourite too. The favourite in the last race was also odds-on. All four horses triumphed at odds of 1/12, 4/11, 7/4 and 4/6 respectively.

However due to the short prices and the poor viewing due to the greyhound track I decided to leave after the third race. The first time I have ever left a racecourse so early by choice.

Friday 17th March - Fakenham

Today is only my third visit to Fakenham races. My last trip her was the corresponding race meeting 18 years ago! 2 ½ hour drive today - M25/M11/A11/A1065. Fakenham racecourse is located adjacent to the superbly named village of Pudding Norton!

In the late 1990's the town was described as "the most boring place on Earth" in "The Knowhere Guide", written by Robert Woods. The comment related specifically to Wednesday afternoons, which is early closing day in Fakenham. The comment was taken and quoted out of context as being 'voted' the most boring place on Earth, and very rapidly the story was running in national newspapers. The town council spent a considerable amount of time, money and effort defending the town trying to prove that this was not the case. Fakenham was recently actually voted to be the seventh best place to live in Britain in Country Life's quality of life survey.

I decided to take a chance on Monfalcone, a multiple Swedish winner in the first race. It never got into the race, travelled at the back of the field throughout and finished a tailed off fourth, 57 lengths behind the third and 72 lengths behind Caprice D'Anglais the 9/4 winner, which led throughout and never looked like beat caught and beat Sailors Warn the 4/6 favourite by 11 lengths.

Little Windmill carried my hopes in the first chase of the day. It led until the twelfth after which it was less than enthusiastic and hit nearly all the remaining fences, eventually finishing a remote fourth, 22 lengths behind the optimistically named Make Me A Fortune, which finished in third place and 43 lengths behind the winner Master Jake, the 3/1 winner. Cabragh the 5/2 favourite came second.

My fortunes improved in the third event as Hint Of Grey was always going well and was nearly 4 lengths clear when it made a mistake at the last but still had enough in hand to beat Cesar Et Rosalie the 8/11 favourite by a length at the line.

I was given a tip for Hallings Comet in the 4 O'clock by a friend so I decided to have a small saver on it. It fell at the first! My selection in the race was Whispering Storm which didn't fare much better. It led and was 3 lengths clear when it blundered 3 out and lost place rapidly and was pulled up at the last.

Rear Admiral carried my money in the second chase of the day. He made a bad mistake at the second fence and was held up in last place, found nothing at the 15th, was left a poor fourth, and eased at the last, finishing 27 lengths behind Beeves the easy 4/1 winner, which forged clear approaching the last and kept on well, beating Fingerontheswitch the 5/2 favourite by 10 lengths.

Tara Mac one of the 3/1 joint favourites was my last hope of the day. It was going reasonably well and went into second at the sixth fence. Things then went downhill. It hit the 11th then fell at the next. By the time D'Nailor, the winner was passing the post I was already in my car and away!

Monday 20th March - Taunton

The first race meeting on the current site at Taunton was held on 21st September 1927. It was the last racecourse to be opened in Britain for 81 years, until Great Leighs (now known as Chelmsford City) racecourse opened in 2008, followed the following year by Ffos Las.

The town name is derived from "Town on the River Tone" - or Tone Town. The town has been the site of many historically important events. During the Second Cornish uprising of 1497, Perkin Warbeck marched a primarily Cornish army approximately 6,000 strong upon Taunton, most of which surrendered to Henry VII on 4th October 1497 in the town. On 20th June 1685 the Duke of Monmouth crowned himself King of England at Taunton during the Monmouth Rebellion. Judge Jeffreys, also known as "the Hanging Judge", lived in the town during the Bloody Assizes which took place in the Great Hall of Taunton Castle.

It is over 32 years since my previous visit to Taunton. Today is only the third time I have been racing here. The weather on the drive down here today was atrocious. It absolutely tipped down en-route. However on arrival I was pleasantly surprised that the going was still good.

Bumped into Steve, a racing acquaintance of mine who lives in Plymouth, who I usually see at York races. We used to stay at the same Bed & Breakfast in York until it changed hands and a Basil Fawlty equivalent took over the premises. In fact after he upset me and I vowed never to stay at his establishment again I sent him a letter telling him he came from the same school of hotel management as Basil! I bet there must have been steam coming out of his ears when he read it. It made me feel better anyway!

The favourite in the opener today, Bags Groove started at the prohibitive odds of 1/3 so I decided to leave the race alone. He duly obliged by six lengths.

I was planning to back High Secret in the second event but only if I could get Even money. He was forecast to be 10/11 favourite but opened at 4/7 on course so I left the race alone. He eventually went off at 4/5, was hard pressed on the run-in and only won by half a length from Boagrius a 5/2 shot which pressed him in the run-in all the way to the line.

I had my first bet of the day, Mr Medic, in third race. He chased the leaders and was challenging for second from the ninth fence before falling back four fences from home and was four lengths behind when he slipped on landing three out and unshipped James Best from the saddle.

Hint Of Mint carried my hopes in the fourth event. He disputed the lead until three flights from home and was only staying on at one pace when he fell two out. Wishfull Dreaming the 7/4 favourite was going well, ½ a length up and looking like the winner until he fell at the last, leaving Amour De Nuit 19 lengths clear of Paddys Runner at the line.

Knights Reward carried my hopes in the fifth race. He was held up in touch, blundered at the second fence and fell four out, giving me my third consecutive non-finisher! Leg Lock Luke, the 2/1 favourite, which had proved to be a costly horse to follow, but with seconds both here and at Exeter was two lengths up and clear after jumping the last. Victory appeared to be assured. However that was not to be, as he veered badly left on the run-in 75 yards from home, snatching defeat from the jaws of victory and unseating Tom O'Brien, handing the race to the lucky backers of Bajardo at 8/1.

Wayne Hutchinson rode Midnight Cowboy, the Alan King runner for me in the final race of the day. However he never really got into the race, staying on one pace to finish third, beaten just over six lengths behind Milord the 11/2 winner.

So off I headed to my B&B in the outskirts of Taunton for the night.

Tuesday 21st March - Exeter

Horse racing has been part of Exeter's heritage since the middle of the 17th century, one of many racecourses created due to Charles II's love of the sport. The racecourse claims to be one of the oldest in the country.

The last duel in Devon occurred at the racecourse in 1833, when Peter Hennis, a doctor, and Sir John Jeffcott, a judge, drew pistols over Henning spreading gossip. Hennis was wounded in the exchange, and died the following week; Jeffcott fled to Sierra Leone.

After a hearty full English breakfast I drove to my friends Cliff & Sue's house in Cullompden, a charming little Devon village roughly half way between Taunton and Exeter. They came racing with me today.

Bumped into Steve again today. He has also been to all the racecourses on the UK mainland, and like me, the last racecourse he visited, before Great Leighs/Chelmsford and Ffos Las recently opened, was Catterick.

Paddocks Lounge was predicted to start around even money in the first race, so I decided to take a chance with Golan Dancer, the 5/2 second favourite. Paddocks Lounge led from the start and kept on well, beating Golan Dancer who finished second, by seven lengths. Sue backed the winner.

Pure Vision provided me with my first winner of the afternoon. He was ridden confidently by Niall Madden, led soon after the last flight and stayed on well to win by three lengths from This Is It the 3/1 favourite.

Galactic Power the 11/2 favourite claimed the prize in the third race, staying on well to beat Boy In A Bentley by 2 ½ lengths. My selection, Martabot lost his place at the sixth before falling back to eventually finish a well beaten fourth, 145 lengths behind the winner.

Clan Des Obeaux started the 4/9 favourite in the first chase of the day which only had a disappointing three runners. I decided to give the race a miss. Drumlee Sunset gave favourite backers a fright as he strongly pressed Clan Des Obeaux four fences from home before being headed between the last two, and finishing 11 lengths behind the winner. Oscars Way a 100/1 shot finished 134 lengths behind to claim the £1,049.40 third prize.

I backed Kap Jazz the 7/4 favourite in the next race. He pressed the leader until the tenth before dropping back to last of the five runners, before eventually overhauling Bindon Mill to finish in third place behind Bertie Boru the9/2 easy winner, which beat Themanfrom Minella by 11 lengths.

Kapgarde King was my selection in the penultimate race of the day. He tracked the leader until being ridden four out, weakening two out, and finishing in fourth position 13 ½ lengths behind Zerachiel the 13/2 winner, which held on close home by a head from Bacchanel the 9/4 favourite.

Canford Chimes, the 7/4 favourite looked like he was going to give Sue her second winner of the day and the bragging rights, before Just A Sting gave me my second winner of the day to overhaul him in the last few strides to win by half a length, and deny Gerard Tumelty a winner in his last ever ride.

A reasonable day at the office in the end for me!

Back to Cliff and Sue's for dinner then back to my B&B for the night.

Wednesday 22nd March - Warwick

The name Warwick means "dwellings by the weir".

Human activity at Warwick dates back to the Neolithic era. Archaeological work on the site of Warwick School (which incidentally claims to be the country's oldest boys' school) in 2017-18 revealed the footings of a sizeable Roman barn from the 2nd century AD. William the Conqueror founded Warwick Castle in 1068 on his way to Yorkshire to deal with rebellion in the north.

Much of the medieval town was destroyed in the Great Fire of Warwick in 1694. Most of the town centre buildings are therefore of late 17th and early 18th century origin, however some medieval timber framed buildings did survive, especially around the edges of the town centre.

Kippers for breakfast for a change today.

I noticed that my good friends Graham and Jan who I have holidayed with in Cape Town for the last ten years had a horse running at Warwick today - Absolutely Frankie in the second race. Rang Graham and they are going as Owners today.

Robbin'hannon which changed hands for £110,000 after winning an Irish point-to-point started favourite in the first event, starting at 9/4 backed in from an opening 11/4. I backed Oscar Boss which was held up in touch in midfield, made some headway around halfway and was in second position until three flights from home. He eventually finished in fifth place 35 ½ lengths behind Robbin'hannon, which stayed on strongly on the flat and won readily by 2 ½ lengths .

Graham's horse, Absolutely Frankie, started one of the two 100/1 rank outsiders in the second race. Multiculture which won by 21 lengths at Wincanton two weeks ago, started the 1/9 favourite. He was never in trouble, and won by 26 lengths. Absolutely Frankie finished fourth, beaten just over 58 lengths, beating one home to claim the £286.20 fourth prize. At least Graham and I got to go into the winner's enclosure to welcome him in.

The third event was only a three horse race. I decided to oppose Krackatoa King, the 8/11 favourite, opting instead for Towering at 11/4. Towering was never going well in last place and was tailed off when he was pulled up at the 15th. Krackatoa King duly obliged favourite backers, beating Timon's Tara with consummate ease by 100 lengths!

Black Narcissus carried my hopes in the fourth race. After being held up in touch and chasing the leaders he hit the third last and weakened afterwards to finish 23 lengths behind The Model County, one of the 7/2 joint favourites.

Sparkling River gave Richard Johnson his fourth winning ride of the day in the following race, asserting after the third last, in command thereafter and eased down on the flat to win by 39 lengths. Listen To The Man, my selection finished fifth, 68 ¼ lengths behind the winner!

I rounded off the day by backing Royals And Rebels, which was soon struggling , lost touch and was pulled up three fences from home. The Last Bridge won the race at 25/1 beating Veauce De Sivola the 5/2 favourite into second place by 20 lengths.

Two days racing at Newbury for me this weekend, then off to the Isles Of Scilly to see my girlfriend, who is busy readying her cottage there for paying guests in a few weeks.

I was originally planning to go racing at Market Rasen next Monday but have now rescheduled it for early June. I am hoping to get back from the Scilly Isles in time to go racing at Wetherby at the end of March.

Friday 31st March - Wetherby

I went racing at Newbury last weekend, which I have already covered as part of my racecourse tour in January. The only reason I mention it here is due to an unfortunate incident which occurred in the Hunter Chase last Friday. Amateur jockey Luke Ridley riding 33/1 shot Lookslikerainted was left well 15 lengths clear of the rest of the field when his only serious challenger Duke Of Lucca (which looked held at the time anyway) blundered and unseated his rider at the last fence. Unfortunately Ridley mistook the ½ furlong marker for the winning post and managed to snatch defeat from the jaws of victory as he eased his mount down and was overtaken by both Triangular and Ballytober. He suffered some verbal abuse from racegoers and received a 28 day ban.

I got back from the Isles of Scilly last night, so off I headed to North Yorkshire today. Caught the train from King's Cross to Leeds, connection to Harrogate then bus to Wetherby. Walked the two miles from Wetherby town centre to the racecourse.

Horse racing in Wetherby first took place on Scaur Bank, In 1891 racing moved to its current location situated off York Road. Wetherby is mentioned in the Domesday Book as Wedrebi, which is thought to mean "settlement on the bend of a river". The town was listed in a recent Sunday Times report as one of the Best Places to live in northern England.

My original selection Quids In, was a non-runner in the opener so I opted for Master Of Finance instead. He tracked Blue Hussar, the leader but had to settle for second place. Blue Hussar won comfortably, by 2 ¼ lengths.

The second race was already underway before I realised I had not had a bet in it. My selection Gin Cobbler was going backwards at the time so I decided not to have a bet in running. He finished a well beaten fourth, nearly 24 lengths behind Chestnut Ben, the 5/1 winner. Bet saved!

Little Bruce, my fancy in the next event, seemed a forlorn hope when he was hampered by a faller 3 out so I put my binoculars down. However miracles do occasionally happen, and Little Bruce came from another county to beat Magic Dancer in the last 50 yards!

I was uncertain whether or not to back Swing Hard, my tentative fancy in the next race so I left it alone. That turned out to be a good decision as he was beaten ¾ of a length by Open Hearted, the Dan Skelton runner. Dan and Harry Skelton, the jockey, are going through a purple patch at the moment, raining and riding nearly 100 winners each this season.

Manwell could only finish a well beaten 9th for me in race 5, over 40 lengths behind Suggestion, the 16/1 winner.

I did not stay for the final two races as I had a bus and two trains to catch. The journey home was good. The bus went through a charming little village called Follifoot. On arrival in York I popped into The Punch Bowl at Micklegate (a JD Wetherspoons pub) for dinner, then popped in to the Trafalgar Bay for a pint of Sam Smith's Old Brewery bitter before catching my train home to London.

Saturday 1st April - Stratford-upon-Avon

Stratford-upon-Avon is a popular tourist destination as it is the birthplace and gravesite of the poet and playwright William Shakespeare and receives around 2.5 million visitors a year.

Stratford was originally by Anglo-Saxons and remained a village until the lord of the manor. John of Coutances created a plan to develop it into a town in 1196. Stratford was granted a charter from King Richard I to hold a weekly market, giving its status as a market town.

During Stratford's early expansion into a town the only way across the river Avon in and out of the town was over a wooden bridge, thought to have been constructed in 1318. However the bridge could not be crossed at times due to the river rising. In 1480 a new masonry bridge was built to replace it called Clopton Bridge, named after Hugh Clopton who paid for its construction.

In 1769 the actor David Garrick staged a major Shakespeare Jubilee over three days which saw the construction of a large rotunda and an influx of many visitors. This contributed to the growing phenomenon of Bardolatry which made Stratford a tourist destination.

A sunny and warm day today. The drive to Stratford took me past another couple of wonderfully named villages, Hampton Lucy and Lower Clopton!

Today is only my second visit to Stratford races. My only previous visit was on 28th May 1977, 14,553 days ago!

An eight race card today as the opening novice hurdle race divided.

Don't Act Up did not start the day well for me, holding no chance throughout the first race and finishing in seventh position, over 31 lengths behind Excellent Team, the easy 11/4 winner.

Quids In, which was a non-runner at Wetherby yesterday was my tentative fancy today in the second race. It was forecast to be the Even Money favourite in the morning paper. It opened at 6/4 and drifted to 15/8. I'll Be Your Clown, an Irish flat import, and now trained by Dan Skelton stable was well fancied and went off the 11/8 favourite. In the end I decided to leave the race alone. Lerichi Belle, a 16/1 shot, gave favourite backers a fright, pressing I'll Be Your Clown all the way to the line, only going down by the shortest of short heads. Quids In was a further 3 ½ lengths behind in third.

I was originally planning to back Astrum in a double with Quids In. Fortunately I did not. I backed Astrum on its own instead. He chased the leader before taking up the running at the fourth obstacle and stayed on well, beating Edgar a 25/1 outsider by 4 lengths.

Pull The Chord held every chance for me in the next race, before making a mistake at the last and weakening on the run-in, and finishing 14 lengths behind Sam Buckle, the 100/30 winner.

St Saviour a 14/1 shot may have been a tad fortunate to win the following race, as Asum the 2/1 favourite was chasing him and only a length down and staying on when he fell at the last. Star Foot, my selection was left second at the last and finished 8 lengths behind the winner.

Viking Mistress raced prominently for most of the following race and looked like the potential winner approaching the turn for home. However he weakened quickly and could only manage 6th in the end, 16 lengths behind North Hill the 100/30 favourite.

Guanciale carried my hopes and a few quid of my cash in the seventh race. He never got into the race and eventually finished last of the seven finishers, 52 lengths behind In On The Act which finished sixth, and nearly 100 lengths behind Modeligo the 6/1 winner.

A nice local racecourse for me next. Ascot tomorrow.

Sunday 2nd April - Ascot

A local course for a change today. By my (admittedly somewhat sketchy) calculations, today is the 3,030th race meeting I have attended, around 480 of which have been at Ascot!

The name Ascot derives from the Old English east and cot (cottage).

Ascot is noted most as the location of Ascot Racecourse, home of the Royal Ascot meeting, and is reportedly one of the most expensive towns in England when taking into account the average house price and the cost of renting a property in the town. The racecourse is owned by the Crown. Royal Ascot is arguably the world's most famous race meeting, dating back to 1711.

Notable residents of Ascot include Chris Evans, Sarah Harding and Marti Pellow. John Lennon and Ringo Starr lived at Tittenhurst Park, Ascot.

Picked up my racing mate Keith at 12:00 and drove to the course, via Windsor Great Park as usual. Today was another lovely sunny and warm spring day.

Enjoyed a couple of pints of real ale before racing, before getting down to the business of trying to pick some winners.

I narrowed the first race down to two, Clondaw Cracker and Tales Of The Tweed. Clondaw Cracker ran like a crab and finished a well beaten last of the 10 runners, 49 ½ lengths behind the winner, Tales Of The Tweed! So I have narrowed my selection down to the winner and the last one home. Now dear reader if you are thinking that I backed Clondaw Cracker you are wrong. I backed the winner! Tales Of The Tweed came with a late rattle to head Springtown Lake, a 33/1 outsider, in the last few strides by ¾ of a length. A good start to the afternoon.

I selected Percy Street, trained by Nicky Henderson and ridden by Nico de Boinville. He was held up towards the back of the field before chasing the leaders after the second last. He tried to close on the leading pair but looked held when he made a mistake at the last. He finished third 4 ¾ lengths behind So Celebre the 9/1 winner who kept on well from the last to beat Dolos by 2 ¾ lengths.

I had planned to back Value At Risk in the third race but he was one of a number of horses withdrawn throughout the afternoon due to the change of going from Good to Good to Firm. I chose Present man instead. He made virtually all the running and was 5 lengths ahead at the last but was all out in the end to win by 1 ¾ lengths.

San Benedito was my fancy in the fourth race. I had some connectivity problems on my mobile phone shortly before the race so I was unsure whether or not my bet on Betfair had been matched so I put a few quid on San Benedito to win on the Tote as he was my nap of the day. He duly obliged, winning comfortably by 7 lengths from Imperial Presence the 2/1 favourite. Clic Work, the Paul Nicholls runner was a length clear when he pecked 2 out, lost his action and pulled up lame. By the way he won I think San Benedito would have won anyway.

Three winners from four bets for me now!

Keith backed Loose Chips, the 12/1 winner in the fifth race, a 3 mile chase. He jumped well throughout, stretching the field from the 15th and outjumping the runner up when challenged 2 out. In the end the post came just in time as he clung on by a fast diminishing head from Bob Tucker, who stayed on well and was gaining at the finish.

My original selection Puffin Billy was another non-runner in the sixth event so I chose Beneagles instead. He was disappointing and never got into the race proper, finishing fifth of the non-runners. Dell' Arca, an 11/1 chance, claimed the prize, staying on well to beat Pilansberg by 1 ¾ lengths.

Monsieur Gibraltar, the favourite in the Hunter Chase which was forecast to be about the 2/1 favourite in the morning paper actually opened at 4/6 and shortened to 8/11. Although we both fancied it, Keith and I decided it was too short to back so we left the course after the sixth race. Monsieur Gibraltar duly obliged, drawing clear from 2 out and winning easily by 9 lengths from Hazy Tom, a 20/1 shot.

I have a busy week's racing planned for next week, starting with Newton Abbot on Tuesday, Aintree on Thursday, Sedgefield on Friday, Chepstow on Saturday and Ffos Las on Sunday (which I have decided to bring forward from July).

Thursday 6th April - Aintree

The name Aintree is thought to be of Saxon origin, meaning "One tree" or "tree standing alone". Local legend held that an oak tree on Bull Bridge Lane (removed in 2004) was the "Ain tree".

Aintree racecourse has staged the Grand National horserace since the 19th Century. There is much debate regarding the first official Grand National, most leading historians now prefer the idea that the first running was in 1836 and was won by The Duke, ridden by Martin Becher. The fence Becher's Brook is named after him and is where he fell in the following year's race. His mount, Conrad, dug his heels in, hurling Becher over his head and into the brook the other side of the fence. Becher lay in the water until the rest of the field had thundered past, before climbing out thoroughly soaked and cursing how he hadn't realised how filthy water tasted without the benefits of whisky.

Contemporary newspaper reports place all the 1836-38 races at Aintree although the 1839 race (won by Lottery) is the first described as "National".

Due to heavy rain on Monday Newton Abbot races were abandoned this Tuesday due to waterlogging. I am now planning to go racing at Newton Abbot on Wednesday 10th May.

Another pleasant dry spring day today. Took 09:07 train from Euston to Liverpool Lime Street then walked the short distance to Liverpool Central and caught a train to Aintree station, which is directly opposite the entrance to the racecourse.

Met my friend Maurice in the Irish Bar and enjoyed a couple of pints of Guinness with him.

A very good card at Aintree today. Winner finding will be difficult with so many good horses to choose from!

Frodon was my selection in the opening race. He led and appeared to be going well until the tenth fence, was headed at the twelfth then went backwards, eventually finishing 45 ½ lengths behind Flying Angel, the 5/1 winner.

I decided to take a chance opposing Defi Du Seuil, the 4/11 favourite, and backing Divin Bere in the Juvenile Hurdle. I got a good run for my money, as Divin Bere tracked the leaders and led the field approaching 2 out but was no match for Defi Du Seuil who won easily, beating Divin Bere by 1 ½ lengths.

The third race had a stellar field: Aso, Bristol De Mai, Cue Card, Empire Of Dirt, Silviniano Conti, Smad Place and Tea For Two. You could make a decent case out for every one of the seven contestants. I chose Empire Of Dirt, who was never travelling and was always at the back of the field and was pulled up lame when tailed off before the third last fence. Tea For Two, ridden by Lizzie Kelly was all out to beat Cue Card by a neck at the line.

Another long odds on favourite in the fourth race - Buveur D'Air. Once again, I decided to take it on, with The New One carrying my hopes. He ran a good race leading until headed approaching the last flight of hurdles and finishing in third position, 6 ½ lengths behind Buveur D'Air the easy winner which was eased down in the closing stages beating My Tent Or Yours by 5 lengths.

I backed Top Cat Henry a 33/1 outsider in the Foxhunters 'Chase run over just over a circuit of the Grand National course. All the other races today were run on the Mildmay course. Top Cat Henry gave me some cause for optimism in the early part of the contest, racing with the leaders, before blundering at Valentines and losing his place. He eventually finished last of the 16 finishers. At least he finished! The other twelve non-finishers Fell (4), Unseated (3) or were Pulled Up (5). Dineur, a 16/1 shot claimed the prize.

I came closest to winning in the 4:40. Theinval raced in midfield and tracked the leaders and taking up the running between the last two fences. Unfortunately he was headed by Double W's, who headed him 75 yards from the post, and beat him by a length at the line.

Not being a fan of bumpers I left the racecourse before the last race, which or the record was won by Dame Rose at 14/1, and headed back to Liverpool for Wetherspoons Curry night before catching the 18:47 Virgin Pendolino train back to Euston and arriving home at 10pm.

Sedgefield is a town and civil parish in County Durham. It had a population of 5,211 as at the 2011 census. A Shrove Tuesday Ball Game takes place in Sedgefield and is an example of Mob Football. Another popular annual event is the Mediaeval Fair which takes place in mid-May, and brings the local community and surrounding areas into the closed central streets of Sedgefield to participate in funfair rides and medieval-themed activities.

Tony Blair, the former Prime Minister was the MP for Sedgefield from 1983 to 2007. In November 2003, Sedgefield was visited by the American president George W. Bush during a state visit. He visited a local pub as well as the local secondary school. This event was preceded by high-intensity security, which included fastening down manhole covers and drains and closing the centre of the village to all traffic. An anti-war protest coincided with his visit, during which president Bush waved cheerily towards some of the protestors, for the benefit of the US media, to try to persuade the American public that he was acknowledging an adoring audience.

Leg 25 of my racecourse tour today and Day 2 of 5 consecutive days horse racing!

Caught a train just after 9 O'clock to York and connecting train to Darlington. I was originally planning to take the bus between Darlington and Sedgefield but the timings were such that I would have missed the first race and have to leave after the fourth race. I decide to rent a car from Darlington instead.   Thank goodness for 21st Century technology, Smart Phones in particular! I booked the car hire, Collision Damage Waiver Excess Insurance and obtained a DVLA Driving Licence check code (required for car hire since the abolition of the paper part of UK driving licences) while I was en-route from Kings Cross to York.

As Sedgefield is part of the Arena Leisure Group of racecourses and I am an annual member at Fontwell Park this year my admission to Sedgefield today, Chepstow tomorrow and Ffos Las on Sunday this weekend are all free. The racecard at Sedgefield was a very reasonably priced £2.00.

Cruising Bye, my selection in the opening 3 ¼ mile chase which was predicted to be the 5/2 favourite in the morning paper drifted like a barge on course, opening at 12/1 and going off at 14/1. The market told the story! Cruising Bye was in touch on the outside of the field until the 17th, after which was outpaced. He finished eighth of the nine finishers (the only other runner was pulled up), 43 ¼ lengths behind Mahler Lad, trained by Donald McCain (son of Ginger McCain who famously trained Red Rum to win three Grand Nationals).

I opposed Cesar Et Rosalie, the 8/11 favourite in the second race, opting instead for the second favourite, Viserion. Viserion led until 3 out however Cesar Et Rosalie kept on well to beat him by 1 ¼ lengths, giving trainer Neil Mulholland his first winner of the day.

Taws was the 1/5 long odds-on favourite in the third race. I thought he was beatable so opted for Stonebrigg Legend instead. I was proved partially correct as Taws was beaten but not by my selection. Louloumills claimed the prize instead, keeping on well to beat Taws by half a length with Stonebrigg Legend a poor third, 21 lengths behind Taws. I must get my ears syringed. During the race I thought I heard the race commentator talking about a 66/1 shot called Bare Arse! On checking the racecard I found that the horse in question was actually called Fair Ask.

My choice in the fourth race, Dark And Dangerous was outpaced for most of the race and was eventually pulled up before 2 out, the race going to The Character, a 9/1 chance.

Neil Mulholland's second winner came in the shape of Master Burridge in the fifth race, giving jockey Mark Quinlan the 125th win of his career in his last ride as a jockey and my only winner of the day. Mark is now going to be Neil Mulholland's assistant trainer.

My selection in the sixth race was Whatdoesthefoxsay. He led until 3 out but was then outpaced, eventually finishing third behind Jac The Legend and Grand Enterprise, the 85/40 favourite.

I did not stay for the seventh race as I had to get my hire car back before the office closed at 6pm and catch my trains back to London.

Saturday 8th April - Chepstow

To advance The ancient Welsh name for Chepstow was Ystraigyl, meaning "a bend in the river". The English name Chepstow derives from the Old English ceap/chepe stow, meaning market place or trading centre.

The oldest site of known habitation at Chepstow is at Thornwell, where recent archaeological investigations revealed continuous occupation from the Mesolithic period of around 5000 BC until the end of the Roman period, about 400 AD. After the Norman conquest of England, Chepstow was a key location. Its position at the lowest bridging point of the river Wye provided a base from which Norman control into south Wales.

Chepstow Castle was founded in 1067, and its Great Tower, often cited as the oldest surviving stone fortification in Britain, dates from around that time. Its site, with sheer cliffs on one side and a natural valley on the other, afforded an excellent defensive location.

Today was the best day of the year weather wise so far. Lovely warm and sunny.

I decided to drive to Chepstow via the beautiful Gloucestershire countryside, which has the additional benefit of not having to pay the exorbitant £6.70 toll to enter Wales on the M4 (it is free in the opposite direction). There is a rumour that the toll will be dramatically reduced (to around £2 in each direction) or even abolished completely when the Severn bridges are returned to public ownership later this year. I will believe that when I see it!

Today was my ninth visit to Chepstow races and my first since December 1999.

My selection in the first race, Top Ville Ben, was predicted to be the 7/4 favourite in this 15 runner contest. I thought that was too short to back so I did not have a bet in the race. Top Ville Ben actually went off the 8/13 favourite and was a length ahead when it fell at the last flight.

Irish Thistle, my fancy in the first chase of the day, was held up towards the rear and lost touch with the leading trio at the tenth , and plugged on to finish a well beaten third, 26 lengths behind the easy 12/1 winner Double Treasure.

Act Four, a 12/1 chance and my selection in the third race, stayed on well under pressure and forged ahead close home to win by 1 ¼ lengths from Bletchley Castle, the 6/5 favourite, giving Ed Bailey, his amateur rider his first ever win.

Back down to earth for me in the fourth race as Petite Power was two lengths down when he fell at the last, victory going to Boa Island at 3/1.

Thundering Home did no such thing for me in the fifth race, finishing a tailed off 11th of the 13 finishers, nearly 40 lengths behind Zulu Oscar, the 11/2 winner who quickened clear in command and eased in the closing stages.

I finished the day backing Lac Sacre, which was always in the last pair and was tailed off when he was pulled up at the 14th fence.

I then watched the Grand National on the big screen, missed the last two races, which were both bumpers, and drove to Llanelli where I was staying the night.

Sunday 9th April - Ffos Las

The Ffos Las area is named after a farm which existed at the site before mining operations began. The English translation of Ffos Las is blue ditch. Ffos Las was the site of an open cast mine between 1983 and 1997, At one time it was the largest open cast mine in Europe and was 500ft deep.

Ffos Las is now best known for Ffos Las racecourse which was completed in 2009 and is built on top of the in-filled open cast mine. Ffos Las racecourse became the first new National Hunt racecourse to be built in the United Kingdom for 80 years.

What a difference a day makes! A cold front brought the temperature right down today and it was a cloudy and chilly day.

I drove the short distance from my overnight digs at Llanelli to Ffos Las racecourse. Today is only my second trip to Ffos Las racecourse, the previous one being six years ago in April 2011, which I recall being a very hot day.

Jameson was sent off a warm favourite at 4/5 in the first race. My selection, Ballyarthur, which was predicted to be the 7/4 favourite in the morning paper, went off at 7/4 but as second favourite. Ballyarthur led until headed 2 out and was left in second position when Kafella fell fatally injured. Ballyarthur plugged on to finish a poor second, 11 lengths behind Jameson who jumped well throughout and won easily.

I had backed Baraza, the 8/11 favourite in a win double with Ballyarthur so left the race alone as I did not fancy backing it at the price. That proved to be a good decision as Looks Like Power, a 9/2 chance, was always holding the odds-on favourite, and beat him by a neck at the line.

Mumper at 10/1 looked like it was going to giver favourite backers a shock, as he led and was going best in the selling chase (the only such race in the 2017 racing calendar). However he made a mistake two fences from home, opening the door for Earthmoves the 4/7 favourite to win by 3 ¼ lengths, somewhat fortunately I think! My selection Hansupfordetroit chased the leaders before dropping back to last of the four finishers, 38 ¼ lengths behind the winner.

Hennli Harri was saddled with my selection in the third chase of the day. He chased the leaders until the 14th but was then ridden and outpaced and plugged on to finish a well beaten third, just over 15 lengths behind Upswing, which just got the better of a battle with Abricot De L'Oasis by a head.

My first success of the afternoon came in the following race. Rocky's Treasure the 100/30 favourite was confidently ridden towards the back of the field before making headway at the ninth and leading 2 out and beating Driftwood Haze comfortably by 3 lengths.

Rocknrollrambo gave me my second success of the day in the 5:00 race. He was held up in touch in rear, led 2 out and won comfortably, beating the always held Bennys Girl by a neck.

I left before the closing event (another bumper) as I had a 3 ½ hour drive home. En-route I saw two signs for Otters Crossing the road! I did not however see any otters crossing the road.

Monday 10th April - Kelso

Day trip to Kelso today. Took the 09:25 BA flight from Heathrow to Newcastle and rented a car.

The town of Kelso came into being as a direct result of the creation of Kelso Abbey in 1128. Sir Walter Scott attended Kelso Grammar School in 1783 and said of the town, "it is the most beautiful if not the most romantic village in Scotland".

For some period of time the Kelso parish was able to levy a tax of 2 pence (2d) on every Scottish pint of ale, beer or porter sold within the town. The power to do this was extended for 21 years in 1802 under the Kelso Two Pennies Act when the money was being used to replace a bridge across the river Tweed that had been destroyed by floods.

Racing first took place at Kelso in 1822. Kelso racecourse is known as "Britain's Friendliest Racecourse".

What is it about Otters? Yesterday it was the Otters Crossing signs on the road near Ffos Las. Today I drove through the village of Otterburn! Fortunately I didn't see any burnt otters today.

Drove along some very winding scenic 'A' roads which looked more like 'B' roads to me. Arrived at Kelso racecourse at 1:20, just under an hour before the first race. A big crowd of racegoers of various ages (not just the usual midweek male pensioners) were in attendance today.

I chose Buckled in the opening 2 ¾ mile hurdle. He was held up in touch and held every chance 2 out before weakening on the run-in and finishing in fifth position, about 5 lengths behind Too Many Chiefs, the 12/1 winner which raced prominently, got outpaced before 2 out then stayed on strongly to win by a length from the runner-up.

Whitsundays carried my money in the next event, the first chase of the day. He raced ion snatches and was outpaced 5 out then rallied after the second last and was 5 lengths clear of the rest of the field at the winning post.

The second chase of the day turned into a virtual match between Scotswell and Nakadam (which won the race last year), who were both well clear of the other runners. Scotswell jumped well throughout and stayed on well to beat Nakadam by 3 ¼ lengths. My selection, Ballyben was prominent in the early stages of the race but got outpace before the 13th fence and was struggling thereafter, finishing seventh of the nine runners nearly 30 lengths behind the winner.

Blue Hussar, who won at Wetherby only tend days ago was forecast to be the 8/'11 favourite. He opened at 4/7 and went off the Even Money favourite (I did hear one bookmaker offering 11/10 just before the off). Blue Hussar did not like value to me in this twelve runner field, together with the fact that he was drifting significantly in the betting, so I decide not to have a bet in the race. He made fairly hard work of it being pressed by Slanelough for most of the final circuit before staying on strongly on the run-in to beat that rival by a length.

Sky Full Of Stars was my pick in the third chase of the day. He raced prominently until 3 out and made no impression thereafter, finishing fourth of the six finishers, 12 ¾ lengths adrift of Welcome Ben, a 12/1 chance, which kept on well to beat Chain Of Beacons, the 11/4 favourite by 2 lengths.

I selected Five Piers, the 5/2 favourite in the Buccleuch Cup (a maiden Hunters' Chase). He made steady headway until the 14th before weakening 2 out and finishing sixth28 lengths behind Havana Jack which led and was going well 3 out and looked the winner from then on.

I selected Surprise Vendor in the Conditional Jockeys' Handicap Hurdle, the final event of the day. He tracked the leaders before fading 4 out. He finished seventh of the ten finishers31 ½ lengths behind Sudski Star, the 10/1 winner, which made virtually all and stayed on strongly to win by 6 lengths.

I managed to back one more loser today as I missed the Car Hire Return sign at Newcastle Airport, and drove into a car park and had to pay £2.50 to get out of it! Hey ho!

Wednesday 12th April - Catterick

Catterick is probably best known for Catterick Garrison located 4.7 miles west of the village. It is the largest British Army garrison in the world with a population of around 13,000 in 2017.

The name Catterick is derived from the Latin place name Cataractonium, which looks like a Latin/Greek mixture meaning "place of a waterfall". However it might have been a Roman misunderstanding of the Celtic name Catu-ratis meaning "battle ramparts".

Catterick prospered as a coaching town where travellers up the Great North Road would stop overnight and refresh themselves and their horses. Today's Angel Inn was once a coaching inn.

Another two stage journey to the races today. Took the 09:08 Virgin Trains East Coast train from King's Cross to York then rented a car from Budget to take me to Catterick races. Catterick was the last racecourse I visited when I completed all the UK mainland racecourses in 1984. Today is my first visit to Catterick since then.

Another bright and sunny day, blustery at times but warm when I managed to get out of the wind at the racecourse. Drove past a signpost to another wonderfully named village, Nun Monkton.

Today was my first turf flat meeting of the new season. My selection in the opener was Wishing Time, one of the joint favourites. He chased the leader, Joysunny, led narrowly 1f out and held on all out to beat him by a fast diminishing head. It crossed my mind that if I stopped betting now for the rest of the flat season, I would have a 100% success record. Of course that was never going to happen.

I narrowed the second race down to two, Kajaki and Surround Sound. I backed Surround Sound. Needless to say Kajaki won the race. Surround Sound finished a one paced fourth, beaten 3 ¾ lengths.

Someone Exciting was saddled with my selection in the third event. He raced in touch and kept on but could only manage fourth place, 3 ¼ lengths behind Bahamian Bird, the 9/1 winner.

I resumed the winning trail courtesy of Fingal's Cave in the 7 furlong claimer. He raced prominently led at the furlong marker and kept on well to beat Victoire De Lyphar by 1 ¾ lengths at the post.

Be Perfect, a 10/1 chance, gave me my third winner of the day in the fifth race. The post came just in time as he was all out to beat Sellingallthetime by a neck at the death.

I never heard Bold Spirit mentioned in running in the sixth race. He finished seventh of the eleven runners, around 3 ½ lengths behind Major Valentine who made all and won well.

Ambitious Icarus raced in midfield in the seventh race and could only manage to finish fifth for me, 3 lengths behind Blue jacket who raced prominently throughout and held off the challenge of Windforpower by a neck.

I finished the day by backing a fourth winner, Kinloch Pride in the closing 5 furlong sprint. She chased the leaders and always looked like holding off the challenge of Culloden, who she beat by a neck.

Next stop Bath on Good Friday.

Friday 14th April - Bath

The city of Bath is renowned for its Roman-built baths. The city became a spa with the Latin name Aquae Sulis "the waters of Sukl" around 60 AD when the Romans built the baths. Hot springs were known even before then. In the 17th century claims were made about the curative properties of water from the springs and Bath became popular as a spa town in the Georgian era. It became a World Heritage site in 1987.

During the English Civil War the city was garrisoned for Charles I. £7,000 was spent on fortifications, but on the appearance of parliamentary forces the gates were thrown open and the city surrendered.

In the 2010 Google Street View Best Streets Awards the Royal Crescent took second place in the "Britain's Most Picturesque Street" award, first place being given to The Shambles in York.

Several foods have an association with the city. Sally Lunn buns (a type of teacake). They can be eaten with sweet or savoury toppings and are sometimes confused with Bath buns, which are smaller, round very sweet and very rich. Bath Olivers, a dry baked biscuit invented by Dr William Oliver, and Bath Chaps, the salted and smoked cheek and jawbones of the pig, also takes its name from the city.

Nightmare journey to Bath today. Left home at 11:05 and didn't arrive at the track until 2:50pm! Heavy Bank Holiday traffic exacerbated by a gas tanker which caught fire and caused the closure of the M4 in both directions between Junctions 17 and 18.

Overcast and chilly day. MASSIVE Bank Holiday crowd of around 9,200 at Bath races today, car park chocker, and £25 Grandstand admission which I thought was a bit steep.

Global Alexander, an 11/4 chance, which I would have backed in the first race, finished second to Esprit De Corps the 7/4 favourite which apparently ran well and won readily by 3 ¼ lengths.

Chatoyer which I would have backed in the second division of the Maiden sprint also went off at 11/4 but was apparently never going the pace and finished fourth, 11 ¼ lengths behind Goodwood Crusader the 6/1 winner, which led entering the final furlong and ran on well by all accounts.

I arrived at the course shortly before the third race. I thought that my selection, Midtech Star was a bit short at 6/4 so I decided not to have a bet in the race. In a close finish Midtech Star held off the strong challenge from EddieMaurice to win by a neck.

I was on the phone to my girlfriend when the fourth race was despatched by the starter, so missed the opportunity to back Sofia's Rock, the 11/4 favourite, which was my selection. He led until headed entering the final furlong and finished in fourth place, a length behind Hushood, the 11/2 winner, which led in the final strides, heading Mister Manduro by a head at the wining post.

Muthmir the 10/11 favourite was too short a price for me to consider backing in the 4:00 race so once again I did not have a bet. He led at the distance and ran on well to beat Mr Lupton by 1 ¼ lengths.

I placed my first bet of the day in the sixth race, Invermere at 14/1. He was held up, made some headway 2 furlongs out before fading in the final furlong. He finished 6 ¼ lengths behind Oh This Is Us at 3/1, which kept on well to beat Hors De Combat, who was closing on him, by a neck.

I came closest to backing a winner today in the 5:00 race. Last Page led entering the final furlong but edged badly left entering the final furlong (which may have cost him the race) and was headed in the final stride by Chagatai, the 7/4 favourite who just caught him. Tara Mitchell (no relation) was the groom who won the cash prize for the Best Turned Out award for Last Page.

I decided to give the last race a miss in order not to get caught in traffic leaving the car park.

My journey home was uneventful and only took 1 ¾ hours to cover the 103 miles, which took over twice as long in the opposite direction.

Saturday 15th April - Musselburgh

Musselburgh is the largest settlement in East Lothian on the Firth of Forth, 5 miles east of Edinburgh city centre and has a population of around 21,900. The name Musselburgh is Old English in origin, with "mussel" referring to the shellfish, and "burgh" derived from the Old English for town.

Musselburgh is known as "The Honest Toun" and celebrates this by the annual election of the Honest Lad and Lass. The town motto "Honestas" dates back to 1332, when the Regent of Scotland, Randolph, Earl of Moray, died in the burgh after a long illness during which he was devotedly cared for by the townsfolk. His successor offered to reward the people for their loyalty but they declined, saying they were only doing their duty. The new regent, the Earl of Mar, was impressed and said they were a set of honest men, hence "Honest Toun".

The Musselburgh Silver Arrow is reputed to be the oldest sporting trophy in the United Kingdom, and is competed for annually by the Royal Company of Archers. It dates back to at least 1603.

I flew up to Edinburgh today then took two buses to get to Musselburgh racecourse. Another enormous Bank Holiday weekend crowd today. It is nearly 16 years since my previous visit to Musselburgh racecourse and I am pleased to say that the facilities have vastly improved. I must not leave it another 16 years before I come racing here again.

My selection in the opening seven furlong handicap was Roll On Rory. He took a keen hold and was in touch until he was outpaced over a furlong out, finishing eighth in the end, 9 ¼ lengths behind Twin Appeal, the 11/2 winner.

Monsieur Joe, the 5/2 favourite, was my fancy in the first of three races over the minimum 5 furlong trip today. He tracked the leaders but was soon outpaced and was well beaten, finishing in fifth position 8 ½ lengths adrift of Desert law, the 14/1 winner, which quickened clear and won readily.

I backed Rashford's Double and had a saver on Mailshot in the Royal Mile Handicap. They came ninth and eleventh respectively. Cullingworth, a 16/1 chance won the race for Sammy Jo Bell, who was having her first winner since coming back from injury, having broken her pelvis in a race at Carlisle in May 2016.

Isharah was my tip in the big race of the day, the inaugural running of the £100,000 Queen's Cup over a mile and three quarters. He came seventh, having raced in midfield and making no impression form a furlong out. Carbon Dating, at 12/1 claimed the prize, running on strongly in the final furlong and mastering my selection by 4 ½ lengths.

I decided to back Requinto Dawn and War Of Succession, both relatively short priced favourites in races five and six in a win double. Requinto Dawn came second, beaten ¾ of a length by Excellently Poised, an 8/1 shot in the fifth race. War Of Succession came third, beaten just over 3 ½ lengths by What's The Story in race six. Fortunately I had a saver on Excellently Poised.

I fancied Royal Brave in the last race and managed to get nearly 6/1 on Betfair about the 4/1 favourite. He tracked the leaders, led inside the final furlong and kept on strongly to beat Enterprising Ben by half a length.

I have now covered 31 of the 61 racecourses so am now just over half way.

Monday 17th April - Redcar

There are about 23 listed buildings in Redcar. At the west end of High Street is a Grade II listed clock tower, a memorial to King Edward VII who was a regular visitor to Redcar. To the east is the listed Church of St Peter, designed by Ignatius Bonomi and built 1822-28.

In the South-East of Redcar is an aircraft listening post built in 1916 during the First World War as part of a regional defence system to detect and give early warning of approaching enemy aircraft, principally Zeppelins. It is an example of an acoustic mirror. The mirror was used up until the invention of radar. It was built on open fields however a modern housing estate now surrounds it. Only the concrete sound mirror remains and is now a Grade II listed building.

Redcar is home to Redcar Royal National Lifeboat Institution (RNLI) station, founded in 1802 making it one of the oldest lifeboat stations in the UK. The RNLI host an annual Lifeboat Day to raise money, with thousands of spectators gathering at the sea front to watch a lifeboat and helicopter display.

Today is my seventh visit to Redcar races but my first in just under 29 years. Long journey involving 3 trains, Kings Cross to York, York to Middlesbrough, Middlesbrough to Redcar Central. Unfortunately the York to Middlesbrough train was delayed so I missed my planned connection to Redcar Central and consequently missed seeing the first race.

Due to the long journey I only planned to stay until the fifth race. Having missed the first I decided to go into the Course enclosure instead of the Grandstand. The viewing was excellent, especially of the straight course which all bar one of today's races were run on. There is also a grass bank in the Course enclosure adding to the visibility of the runners.

Loads of ankle biters today as it is Easter Monday Bank Holiday.

I kept tracked of my selection, Kinloch Pride (which won for me in the last race at Catterick last week) in the opener while I was en-route on the train, on Betfair where I had placed my bet. At one stage in running he went odds-on; however Carlton Frankie, the 2/1 favourite overhauled him in the final furlong and won a shade cosily in the end, beating Kinloch Pride by a length.

I backed Ninepin Bowler and had a saver on Mellor Brook in the first division of the Happy Easter Maiden Stakes. Ninepin Bowler chased the leaders and kept on inside the final furlong finishing fourth, a neck behind my other fancy which also kept on but was short of room towards the finish. Carigrad an 11/4 chance won the race by a neck from Armandihan, the 9/4 favourite, which was headed near the finish.

My nap of the day was Playwriter in the second division of the Happy Easter Maiden. He dwelt, took a ken hold towards the back of the field, made some reasonable headway but did not have the pace to challenge the leaders, finishing in third place, 5 ¼ lengths behind Everything For You, one of the 11/4 joint favourites. Triangulate, a 250/1 rank outsider belied his odds and finished fourth, his groom winning the prize for the best turned out.

Wentworth Falls, the winner of the first 6 furlong race of the afternoon had sprung a 33/1 surprise win in his previous race at Doncaster on 2nd April. That was obviously no fluke as he went off the 9/2 favourite today and kept on well to beat Tiger Jim by half a length. My selection, Musharrif was with the leader until ridden 3 furlongs out, weakened a furlong from home and finished ninth.

My final bet of the day was Imperial Focus in the 4:20. He pressed the leader until ridden 2 furlongs out then faded to finish last of the ten runners, behind Roller, the 3/1 favourite, who won readily by 2 lengths, and was eased well inside the final furlong.

I caught the 16:43 train from Redcar Central to Middlesbrough then had a half hour wait for my connection to York. Interesting to discover that Middlesbrough railway station is actually a Grade 2 listed building. It was designed by the wonderfully named railway architect William Peachey, completed in 1877 and was extensively damaged by bombing during World War 2.

There is also a plaque to the equally unusually named Ralph Bottom at Middlesbrough station. He was a Works Officer for British Rail and co-ordinated environmental improvements at the station between 1984 and 1990. History lesson over.

I managed to find time to pop into the Punch Bowl pub at Micklegate in York for a pint and a bite to eat before catching my train home. Unfortunately I had to stand all the way to London as I did not have seat reservation and the train was completely full as it was the end of the Bank Holiday weekend and lots of passengers had to stand in the aisles and vestibules.

Tuesday 18th April - Newmarket (Rowley Mile Course)

The turf flat racing season 'proper' starts today with the Craven meeting at Newmarket today.

Took the 11:44 train to Cambridge, connecting train to Newmarket and courtesy coach to Newmarket.

Newmarket is generally considered to be the birthplace and global centre of thoroughbred horse racing. It is the largest racehorse training centre in Britain and the largest racehorse breeding centre in the country. The town has had close royal connections since the time of James I, who built a palace there and was a base for Charles I, Charles II and many monarchs since.

Newmarket has over 50 horse training stables, two large racecourses, the Rowley Mile and the July Course, and one of the most extensive and prestigious horse training grounds in the world. The town is home to over 3,500 racehorses, and it is estimated that one in every three local jobs is related to horse racing. Newmarket also is home to the National Horseracing Museum, Tattersalls racehorse auctioneers, and two of the world's foremost equine hospitals.

Racing at Newmarket has been dated as far back as 1174. The town is also home to the PGI Protected Newmarket sausage. Produced since the 1880s, three local butchers in the town are entitled to produce these unique flavoured sausages. The sausages are given as a prize for the Newmarket Town Plate held each year in the town.

Down to the action. The Wood Ditton stakes is always a tricky one as the race is for 3 year olds which have never run. I usually go for a horse from a top stable which cost a lot of money! As the Sheikh Hamdan Al Maktoum horses are usually race fit and in with a chance I chose Dawaaleeb which was carrying their black cap (as opposed to the striped cap of their first colours) and normally is a better price, as was the case today. Dawaaleeb started at 10/1 whereas Elyaasaat was the 7/4 favourite. Dawaaleeb chased the leaders until he was unable to quicken 2 furlongs out and finished fifth, 8 ¼ lengths behind Night Circus the 13/2 winner. Elyaasaat finished sixth.

My main selection the second race was Sound And Silence, the Godolphin horse, ridden by William Buick. I also had a sneaking fancy for Frozen Angel, so had a little saver on that too. Sound And Silence and Never Back Down fought out the finish with Sound And Silence running on well and holding him off by half a length at the line. Frozen Angel dwelt, ran green in at the back of the field and never got in a blow and came last of the nine runners.

I took a chance with Mitigate, a 25/1 shot in the 2:55. He was held up at the back of the field, was soon struggling and outpaced and finished last of the six runners. Beat The Bank at 7/1 stayed on well in the final furlong to beat Salsabeel, the 5/4 Godolphin owned and Charlie Appleby trained favourite.

I backed Repercussion, a French import in the fourth race. He raced in mid division without threatening the leaders, finishing sixth of the thirteen runners, beaten 4 ½ lengths behind Next Stage, a 4/1 chance owned by Godolphin and trained by Saeed bin Suroor.

Khalidi, trained by John Gosden and ridden by Frankie Dettori carried my money in the fifth race. In a close finish Khalidi prevailed from Salouen the 5/2 favourite by a neck.

Mukalal, another Hamdan al Maktoum horse was by choice in the sixth event. He chased the leaders and had every chance 2 furlongs out but was unable to quicken and was beaten a furlong out. He finished fifth of the nine runners, 6 ¼ lengths behind Jewel House at 15/2. Firefright, the 7/4 favourite finished third beaten 2 lengths.

I decided to give the 5:05 race a miss in order to catch the 5:17 train from Newmarket.

Next stop Cheltenham on Thursday.

Thursday 20th April - Cheltenham

Cheltenham is a large spa town on the edge of the Cotswolds and became known as a health and holiday resort following the discovery of mineral springs in 1716. Cheltenham also hosts various festivals including the Cheltenham Literature Festival, Cheltenham Jazz Festival, Cheltenham Science Festival, Cheltenham Music Festival, Cheltenham Cricket Festival, Cheltenham Food & Drink Festival and of course, the Cheltenham National Hunt Festival, held in March every year, the highlight of which being the Cheltenham Gold Cup.

Cheltenham stands on the small river Chelt, which rises at nearby Dowdeswell and runs through the town on its ways to the Severn. It was first recorded in 803 as Celtan hom, which preserves the pre-British noun cilta meaning "steep hill, referring here to the Cotswold scarp; the second element may mean "settlement" or "water-meadow".

Horse racing at Cheltenham Racecourse began in 1815, in the nearby village of Prestbury, and is home of National Hunt racing in the UK. Its popularity increased after the Festival was established in 1902. The racecourse attracts tens of thousands of visitors to each day of the festival every year.

Leg 34 today. Met my friend Keith and saw another friend called Bob at Paddington station. Caught the 10:30 train to Swindon, connecting train to Cheltenham Spa, then a local bus to Cheltenham racecourse.

Started the day well. My selection in the first race, Brillare Momento, which I managed to back at 10/1 beat Dusky Legend one of the 2/1 joint favourites by a neck in the final strides. Brillare Momento was ridden before the last flight, hit it and was headed then rallied gamely to get up just before the post.

I fancied Antartica De Thaix in the second race, However it drifted significantly in the betting from 13/8 to 9/4 causing me to have reservations about backing it so I left the race alone. Antartica De Thaix led and was up to 8 lengths clear at times before being headed 2 out then fell back to finish a well beaten fourth, beaten 15 ¼ lengths behind Plaisir D'Amour which came home 6 lengths clear of the runner up.

Carnspindle carried the Mitchell money in the third race. He raced prominently, was pushed along 2 out, kept on gamely but could only finish second to Midnight Tour, the 9/4 Alan King trained and Davy Russell ridden favourite.

Aidan Coleman rode his third winner of the day in the fourth race, Upswing the 4/1favourite and I backed it. He was held up confidently in rear, was still in fifth place 2 out, led at the last and quickly asserted to win by 2 ½ lengths.

Mr Clarkson was my selection in the fifth event. He raced in midfield, was driven 2 out and was well beaten before the last, 25 ½ lengths behind Two Swallows the 13/2 winner, which stayed on gamely to lead close home, prevailing by ½ a length from Rolling Maul which was worn down close home.

Swincombe Scorchio carried my money in the sixth race. He made several mistakes throughout the race and plodded home last of the four finishers, 18 ¾ lengths behind Fact Of The Matter, the 9/2 winner. Four horses either fell or unseated their riders in the race, one of which was Ten Sixty, the 3/1 favourite. Great call by the racecourse commentator "Ten Sixty passed the winning post. Just a circuit too early and no rider!".

Keith and I left before the bumper and a charity race, caught a bus back to Cheltenham town centre and popped into The Bank House, a JD Wetherspoon's pub for a curry and a pint before catching our train back to Paddington.

Monday 24th April - Pontefract

At the end of the 11th century, the modern township of Pontefract consisted of two distinct and separate localities known as Tanshelf and Kirkby. The 11th century historian Orderic Vitalis recorded that, in 1069, William the Conqueror travelled across Yorkshire to put down an uprising which had sacked York, but that, upon his journey to the city he discovered that the crossing of the River Aire, at what is now Pontefract had been blockaded by a group of Anglo-Scandinavian insurgents, who had broken the bridge and held the opposite bank. Such a crossing point would have been important in the town's early days, providing access between Pontefract and other settlements in the north and east, such as York. Historians believe that, in all probability, it is this historical event which gave the township of Pontefract its modern name. The name Pontefract originates from the Latin for "broken bridge", formed of the elements pons ("bridge") and fractus ("broken").

Pontefract's deep sandy soil makes it one of the few places in Britain in which liquorice can successfully be grown. The town has a liquorice-sweet industry, and the famous Pontefract cakes are produced, although the liquorice plant itself is no longer grown there.

It is nearly 24 years since my last visit to Pontefract races. Today is my 3rd.

Travelled by train to Pontefract Tanshelf station changing at both Wakefield Westgate and Wakefield Kirkgate stations then just over a ten minute walk to the track.

I could only vaguely recollect Pontefract racecourse. It is a left handed course with a sharp turn into the straight just over a quarter of a mile from the winning post. I was generally impressed with the stands and other facilities, including the newly refurbished parade ring.

Down to business. My selection in the opening five furlong sprint was Sinaloa, the 2/1 favourite. It was drawn 1, the plum draw here, but dwelt at the start, tracked the leaders and made some headway on the inner. He stayed on in the final furlong but was unable to get to Gisele's Angel which was quickly away and stayed on strongly to win by a length from Lord Riddiford, a 16/1 chance, with Sinaloa a further head behind in third.

In the second race my fancy, Rockwood raced in midfield and kept on in the final furlong but only managed to finish in fifth spot, 4 ¾ lengths behind Red Tea, the 4/1 favourite which was ridden clear in the final furlong and stayed on strongly to prevail by 2 ¼ lengths from the runner-up.

My choice in the third race was Art Collection. He was held up and was soon detached at the back of the field, eventually finishing sixth of the seven runners, 4 ¾ lengths adrift from Judicial, who quickened well to beat Edward Lewis, the 7/4 favourite by 1 ½ lengths.

My selection in the Pontefract Marathon run over nearly 2 ¾ mile, was La Fritillaire, the 5/2 favourite. He tracked the leaders and took the lead just over 2 furlongs out but was soon driven and beaten. He finished sixth, 12 lengths behind Tuscan Gold, who won the tussle with Madam Lilibet in the final 100 yards, the pair of them 8 lengths clear of Riptide which finished third.

I hedged my bets in the fifth race, backing both Hitchcock at 4/1 and Noble Sword a 33/1 outsider. Hitchcock raced in touch, was carried right a furlong out and was one paced after, finishing in fifth 6 ½ lengths behind Black Isle Boy the 5/1 winner which led a furlong out and stayed on well to win by 1 ¾ lengths from Wild Acclaim. Noble Sword was always towards the rear but did manage to finish sixth, ¾ of a length behind Hitchcock. Star Catch the 5/4 favourite finished last of the nine runners!

Henley, my fancy in the sixth event fared better than my selections in the earlier races, finishing second, 2 ¾ lengths behind Oriental Relation. Things did not improve thereafter! Sakurajima could only finish 7th of the 8 runners behind Alfred Richardson in the 7th race, only a nose ahead of the last horse home.   Reinstorm could only manage to finish fifth of the eight runners in the last race, 8 ½ lengths behind Miss Sheridan the 7/2 favourite.

8 races, 9 bets and 0 winners! Hopefully I will fare better at Epsom on Wednesday.

Wednesday 26ʰ April - Epsom

Epsom Downs Racecourse is of course, famous for holding The Derby, now a general term given for local rivalries in various sports competitions in English-speaking countries. The Derby originated at a celebration following the first running of the Oaks Stakes in 1779. A new race was planned, and it was decided that it should be named after either the host of the party, the 12th Earl of Derby, or one of his guests, Sir Charles Bunbury. According to legend the decision was made on the toss of a coin, but it is probable that Bunbury, the Steward of the Jockey Club, deferred to his host.

The British Prime Minister Lord Rosebery, was sent down (expelled) from the University of Oxford in 1869 for buying a racehorse and entering it in the Derby. It finished last!

For many years the Derby was run on a Wednesday or a Thursday and on the day huge crowds would come from London, not only to see the race but to enjoy a funfair. During some of the 19th and most of the 20th century, Parliament would adjourn to allow members to attend the meeting.

The town also gives its name to Epsom salts, originally extracted from mineral waters here.

Closer to home today. Took the tube to Victoria then mainline train to East Croydon and Tattenham Corner. Met my racing mate Keith at the racecourse and enjoyed a few pints of Guinness with him over the course of the first four races.

I must admit I was not exactly brimming with confidence with my selections today. A difficult card.

My choice in the opening 5 furlong sprint was Majestic Hero. He was held up in touch in midfield, was shaken up to challenge a furlong out and took up the running well inside the final furlong and ran on well to win by a comfortable ¾ of a length.

I decided to back Cracksman and Galapiat, the 4/6 and 11/10 favourites in races 2 and 3 in a double. John Gosden has trained the winner of the second race four times in the previous ten years. Cracksman started a hot favourite but made very hard work of it and looked beaten approaching the final furlong. However he knuckled down and ran on well and just caught Permian in the last stride. Galapiat ran a lot better, making all, quickened 3 furlongs out and ran on strongly to beat Whinging Willie, a 25/1 shot by 4 ½ lengths in a facile victory.

In race four Innocent Touch, my selection was held up in midfield but made no impression on the leaders and finished 7th of the 11 runners, 5 lengths behind Brorocco, the 7/1 winner.

I decided to leave Leader's Legacy, the Godolphin horse, alone in the fifth race as I thought it was a bit too short at 11/8 favourite. He chased the leaders and took up the running a furlong out and was soon clear, ran on strongly and won easily by 4 lengths from Romanor, the 12/1 runner-up.

I backed Vantage Point, the 7/2 favourite in the last race. He raced in touch in midfield, kept on inside the final furlong but could only manage fifth, 6 ¼ lengths behind Emenem, the 9/1 winner.

Five bets and three winners. A good result today.

Off to Scotland for the day tomorrow!

Thursday 27th April - Perth

The classic definition of Perth has been as a city, and traditional documentation confirms that this has been true since time immemorial. In the late 1990s, the UK Government and the devolved Scottish Executive re-examined the definition of a city and produced a list of approved cities, from which Perth was omitted. Despite this, road signs around the borders used the term "The City of Perth", and directional signs within indicated "City Centre".

In June 2007, Alex Salmond, the then First Minister of Scotland, backed a campaign to confer city status on Perth. Perth was one of the 26 bidders for city status to mark the Queen's Diamond Jubilee in 20912. On 14 March 2012, Perth's city status was successfully reinstated.

Perth in Australia and Perth in Canada are both named after Perth in Scotland.

Almost a disaster of a day! Caught 10:00 BA flight from Heathrow to Glasgow. Arrived 10 minutes late and walked to Car Hire area only to discover that the Car Hire company I had booked with does not have a desk there. Read my email from them and found out that they operate from an off airport site so they had to send a shuttle bus to collect me.

When I arrived at their location, to my surprise the Car Hire company said they needed a recent utility bill as proof of my address in addition to my driving licence and DVLA check code. This information was in my email from them. I just had not read it. Things were not looking good! I had visions of having to ring a friend of mine in Glasgow and going drinking with him for most of the day. As it happened that would have been a less stressful option that how the rest of the day panned out!

Fortunately I was given the option for the car hire company to conduct a credit check on me, for a small additional charge, to verify my home address to their satisfaction. Incidentally the car hire company wanted £37 (twice the cost of the actual car hire!) to cover the £1,250 Collision Damage Waiver excess. Fortunately I had paid for this independently for a much more reasonably £1.89. I eventually drove off at 12:45. The first race at Perth, 71 miles away was at 2pm, so I was never going to make that as the driving time according to Google Maps was about an hour and a half.

Lovely drive through the scenic Scottish countryside and past a sign to another wonderfully named village called Findo Gask. The woodlands around this small village just off the A9 are renowned as an excellent site for the collection of black truffles, and truffle hunters are often observed there.

I arrived at Perth racecourse at 2:10 pm, in good time for the second race. I had not been able to obtain a copy of the Racing Post locally or at Heathrow airport so had not been able to make any selections before I got to the racecourse. I could not find a Racing Post salesman at Perth and most of the form from Perth was missing in the betting shop so I had to 'wing it' by making selections based on the summaries for each horse printed in the racecard.

I probably would not have had a bet in the first race as the favourite was predicted to be too short for me to consider backing. Top Ville Ben opened at 8/13 and drifted to 5/6 before going off the 4/5 favourite in the opener. He finished fourth, nearly 20 lengths behind Ramonex.

In the first race I was able to watch (race 2) I back Valseur Du Granval, at 5/2 which eventually started the 2/1 favourite. He was held up in last place and made some headway before getting outpaced before 2 fences from home and finishing 12 lengths behind Pain Au Chocolat, the 5/2 winner, which kept on well and beat the runner up by 4 lengths.

I backed Mash Potato in the next race. He was held up and was pushed along after 3 out and was outpaced thereafter, finishing fifth 19 ½ lengths behind Bahrikate the 33/1 winner.

I fared slightly better in the fourth race. My selection, Chain Of Beacons made steady headway four fences from home but was left a modest third after the next obstacle and made no impression from 2 out, finishing third, 19 lengths behind Endless Credit, another outsider at 16/1.

I got a bit closer to having a winner in the fifth race with Special Catch at 10/1. He made steady headway to chase the winner 3 out but kept on same pace from the last. Mystifiable won the race, beating Special Catch by 2 ½ lengths at the post. Great comment from the racecourse announcer at one point during the contest of "They are racing two by two in Noah's Ark formation".

I decided to beat the traffic which would be leaving the racecourse after the last race, by making the sixth race the last one I would stay for. That proved to be my best decision of the day. More shortly. Total Assets, my selection raced prominently and led 3 out but was headed approaching the last and went down by ½ a length to Sun Cloud, an 8/1 chance.

The first half hour or so of my drive back towards Glasgow Airport was uneventful. I then got caught up in a traffic jam on the M80 for over an hour. Time ticked on and I was often at a standstill. I had visions of having to spend a night in Glasgow.

The journey back to the car hire location took 3 hours in total. I arrived there just before 8pm. My flight was scheduled to leave at 8:30 and I still had to be driven to the airport, go through security, and get to my departure gate which according to my boarding pass which I had printed the previous day, was due to close at 8:10.

After I had gone through security, I noticed on the departure screens that my flight was at Last Call. I arrived at the gate at 8:15pm, was last onboard and the plane door was closed shortly after I got on.

Made it!

Had two ½ bottles of Sauvignon Blanc on the flight.

Got home at 11pm.

Off to Sandown Park tomorrow and Saturday before resuming the tour at Windsor on Bank Holiday Monday.

Monday 1st May - Windsor

Bank Holiday Monday today and a local racecourse for me today for a change. Only 17 miles and a 33 minute drive from home according to Google Maps. Of course that is never the way things go! Journey took closer to an hour due to a four car accident on the A332 south of Junction 6 of the M4 which reduce the carriageway from two lanes to one. Nevertheless I managed to arrive at the racecourse 40 minutes before the first race.

Windsor is an historic market town. Windlesora is first mentioned in the Anglo-Saxon Chronicle. The name originates from old English Windles-ore or 'winch by the riverside'. By the late 12th century the settlement at Windlesora had been renamed Old Windsor, The village of Old Windsor, just over 2 miles to the south of what is now Windsor, predates it by around 300 years. In the past Windsor was formally referred to as New Windsor to distinguish the two. It is well known as the site of Windsor Castle, one of the official residences of the British Royal Family.

Most of the current town's streets date from the mid to late 19th century. However the main street, Peascod Street is very ancient, predating the castle by many years, and probably of Saxon origin. "New Windsor" was officially renamed "Windsor" in 1974.

I took a chance with Flowing Clarets, a 20/1 outsider in the 2:00 six furlong sprint. She chased the leaders until two furlongs out before weakening quickly to finish last of the ten runners, 13 ¾ lengths behind Picket Line, which just held off the challenge of Viva Verglas by a nose in a driving finish.

King Of Spin, my pick the second race tracked the leaders against the nearside rail 2 furlongs out, was driven and asserted inside the final furlong to win by 1 ½ lengths from Goring.

Due to some finger trouble on Betfair I managed to back Cool Team for 11 times my intended stake! Fortunately I spotted this major error before the third race, and as luck would have it, the price had contracted by nearly a point so I managed to cash out my bet and lock in a small profit. This proved to be even more fortuitous as Cool Team, having closed to challenge a furlong out, did not quicken in the final 100 yards and finished second to Desert Dream by half a length. Phew!

I backed Wind In My Sails, the 4/1 favourite in the fourth race. He broke badly and was held up at the back of the field for most of the race, was shaken up 2 furlongs out but made no real progress and finished seventh of the nine runners7 ¾ lengths behind Secret Art, the9/1 winner, which led in the last 150 yards and stayed on well to win by 1 ½ lengths.

There is a racegoer who once pointed out you cannot miss, who my friends and I refer to as 'The Bin Man'. He is an annual member at Newbury, Sandown Park and Windsor racecourses and seems to spend all afternoon rummaging through bins to find discarded betting slips in the hope of finding winners that other racegoers have accidentally discarded. In America people like him are known as 'swoops'. In Australia they are known as 'Racecourse Emus' (for fairly obvious reasons). In both jurisdictions such people are ejected from racecourses. Unfortunately we do not do so in this country. After the 3:45 race today I saw him pick up £20 from a rails bookmaker. I would have good money on him having not backed that horse!

I backed Cape Banjo, the 3/1 favourite in the 4:20, a mile and a quarter handicap. He chased the leaders until 2 furlongs out, after which he weakened to finish fourth9 lengths behind Solo Hunter, the 12/1 winner, which just managed to hold off the late challenge of Get Back In Paris on the line.

The 4:55 had two non-runners so turned into a three runner race. I fancied Sternruben, which had been running well over the sticks during the winter, but not at 5/4 so I left the race alone. In fact I left before the race to get a head start on the traffic, and weather which was beginning to look threatening. On the drive home the heavens opened. Good call!

I got home in good time to watch the 5:30 five furlong sprint on At The Races, in which Fethiye Boy, a 25/1 outsider held on to a dwindling lead and finished a length in front of my bet, Midnightly by a length, with Monteamiata splitting the pair of them.

Tuesday 2nd May - Nottingham

The settlement which has grown into what is now the city of Nottingham dates back to Anglo-Saxon times or earlier. When it fell under the rule of a Saxon chieftain named Snot it became known as "Snotingaham", the homestead of Snot's people (-inga = the people of;, -ham = homestead).

Nottingham Castle was constructed in 1068. On the return of Richard the Lionheart from the Crusades, the castle was occupied by supporters of Prince John, including the Sheriff of Nottingham. It was besieged by Richard and, after a sharp conflict, was captured. In the legends of Robin Hood, Nottingham Castles is the scene of the final showdown between the Sheriff and the hero outlaw.

In the sporting world, Nottingham is home to the world's oldest professional football club, Notts County, which was formed in 1862. On 11th December 2015, Nottingham was named a "City of Literature" by UNESCO, joining Dublin. Edinburgh, Melbourne and Prague, as one of only a handful in the world. The title reflects Nottingham's literary heritage, with Lord Byron, D.H. Lawrence and Alan Sillitoe having links to the city, as well as a contemporary literary community, a publishing industry and a poetry scene.

It is just over 25 years since my last trip to Nottingham races aka Colwick Park. Today is my third visit here. Travelled by train from St Pancras to Nottingham station First Class today then took the Nottingham Community Transport Ecolink bus to the racecourse. An interesting fact about Nottingham racecourse is that a triple dead-heat happened here in April 2013, only the second time such an event had occurred in over a decade.

Passed a sign to yet another unusually named village, Ratcliffe-on-Soar. Its population in the 2011 census was measured at 141. The village does not have any shops however it does have a church and a marina which is often affected by severe flooding as it is built on a designated floodplain.

My selection in the 2:10 race was Aquadabra, the 5/2 favourite. She raced centre field and was in the lead 2 furlongs out but faded in the final furlong and finished third beaten 2 ¼ lengths to Main Desire, who led a furlong out and won readily.

I always like backing Sheikh Hamdan Al Maktoum's horses as they are usually race fit and rarely run a bad race. Khitaamy was however friendless in the market and started at 25/1. Nobody told the horse though that he was unfancied and he raced prominently throughout and looked the potential winner as he was still in the lead a furlong out. However he was soon ridden and headed but still managed to finish in third place, only 1 ¾ lengths behind Meteor Light, the 7/2 winner.

I backed Scribner Creek, a 7/2 chance in the third race. He was held up in rear and made some headway to chase the leaders 3 furlongs out before being ridden 2 furlongs out and keeping on under pressure to finish fourth, 4 lengths behind Thaqaafa, the 11/4 favourite which stayed on strongly in the final furlong to win by 1 ½ lengths. Another great comment from the racecourse commentator, Stewart Machin after the race "The handicapper's favourite theme tune is The Only Way is up".

I backed La Casa Tarifa, the short 5/4 favourite in the fourth race in a double with Carlton Frankie, which ended up the 6/4 favourite in the seventh race. La Casa Tarifa was very slowly away and lost 15 lengths at the start, was always behind and finished last of the 5 runners, 13 ½ lengths behind Normandie Lady, the 4/1 winner, which led approaching the final furlong and was soon clear of Lincoln Rocks, the runner up, beating him by a comfortable 3 ¾ lengths.

I didn't fare any better in the fifth race as my section, Midnight Vixen, finished last of the ten runners, having led early on.

As the first half of my win double had lost, and Carlton Frankie looked like he might be too short for me to back in the last race, I decide to make the sixth race my last of the day. Brigadoon led and was first past the post (the first time) and kept on well throughout the race before giving way to On Fire, the 2/1 favourite inside the final furlong and only going down by half a length. My best result of the day, if you discount Carlton Frankie which won the last race without any of my money on her!

Goodwood next on Saturday, which will be my 40th racecourse on the tour.

Saturday 6th May - Goodwood

Goodwood House is a country house and estate covering 12,000 acres and is the seat of the Duke of Richmond. The house was built around 1600 and is a Grade I listed building. The house and its grounds are the site of the annual Goodwood Festival of Speed, whilst elsewhere on the estate the Goodwood Circuit motorsport track hosts the annual Goodwood Revival. Goodwood Racecourse hosts "Glorious Goodwood" and a number of other horse race meetings. The estate includes two golf courses and a cricket pitch, home to Goodwood Cricket Club, and a hotel. The headquarters of Rolls Royce Motor Cars is on the Estate.

A half decent day today weather-wise. Took 2 ½ hours to drive here today. Drove near or past a few more unusual place names – Bepton Harting, Cocking and Cucumber Farm and through the beautiful and historic market town of Midhurst. The name Midhurst means "Middle wooded hill" or "place among the wooded hills". The name is derived from the Old English words midd or mid, meaning "in the middle" and hyrst, "a wooded hill". The Norman St. Ann's Castle, dating from about 1120 (only the foundations of which remain), the parish church of St. Mary Magdalene and St. Denis, together with South Pond, the former fish-pond for the castle are the only three structures left from this early period.

Met a few racing friends at Goodwood today – Alan, Barbara and Maurice. Advised Maurice Keith and my travel details for a short trip we will be taking to Stirling which will include 2 days racing at Perth towards the end of September, as he is planning to join us.

An eight race card today. My selection in the first race, Miss Tiger Lily chased the leader until 6 furlongs out, weakened 3 f out and finished 12th of the 14 runners, 16 lengths behind October Storm which swept into the lead 150 yards out and was soon clear, winning by 3 lengths.

Dubka, the 11/4 favourite was my choice in the second event. She tracked the leading pair, was pushed along but did not quicken and was already beaten when impeded a furlong out, then weakened to finish sixth, 11 ¾ lengths behind Ajman Princess, the 6/1 winner which was shaken up and drew well clear over a furlong out, flashing her tail when ridden but in no danger and won by 5 lengths.

My selection the third race was Zwayyan, the 7/2 favourite. He was held up in midfield, shaken up and did not quicken 2 furlongs out, made no progress and eased in the final 75 yards. He finished 11th of the 15 runners, 8 lengths behind Gossiping, the 25/1 winner.

I backed Stepper Point in the 5 furlong sprint. He disputed the lead until hallway before weakening well over a furlong out and finished in eighth position, 9 lengths adrift from Vibrant Chords, which stayed on well in the final furlong and won readily by ¾ of a length from the runner-up.

Intimation carried my money in the fifth race. He tracked the leaders, was shaken up to take second well over a furlong out, but stood no chance with Laugh Aloud, the easy winner, which made all and stretched clear 2 furlongs out and stayed on strongly to win by 3 ¼ lengths.

I did not have a bet in the sixth race as Queen Of Time was predicted to be unbackable and to start at about 1/2 In the event she opened at 10/11 and drifted to 6/5 before coming in to 4/5 at the off. She dwelt slightly at the start as her blindfold came off slightly late. She was held up in fifth, made progress 3 furlongs out, and was shaken up to lead over a furlong out. She stayed on well, and was always holding the runner-up and won by 1 ¼ lengths.

As it was a busy day, I decided to make the seventh race my last. My selection, Dominating tracked the leaders before losing its place badly 3 furlongs out and was struggling thereafter, finishing sixth, 6 ½ lengths behind Road To Dubai.

I did have a bet on Betfair in the eighth race, Arab Moon, which won the 5:20 at Lingfield yesterday. Unfortunately it could not repeat that feat and finished fifth today, having been ridden in touch in midfield before keeping on one pace and never able to threaten Darkroom Angel, the 6/1 winner and finishing 4 ½ lengths behind him.

I am going racing at Newmarket tomorrow for the 1,000 Guineas before resuming my racecourse tour at Ayr on Monday.

The name Ayr can be traced back to a pre-Celtic word meaning watercourse or strong river. In 1197, King William the Lion ordered that a new castle be built between the River Ayr and the River Doon. Ayr was later established as a royal burgh and market town. The King gifted fishing rights to the burgh for the River Ayr and the River Doon in 1236.

Ayr was continuously hit by a number of plagues from 1545 to 1647, resulting in the town's port being quarantined and plague victims being removed from the town on pain of death. In 1652, the town was used as a base and fortress for some of Oliver Cromwell's men. They established a large fortress along the mouth of the River Ayr and erected walls around the area, most of which remain to the present day.

A brilliant sunny and warm day today. Not a cloud in the sky! My seventh time racing at Ayr today, but my first in 22 years. Horse racing at Ayr dates back to 1576 but the first official meeting did not take place until 1771. In the early days, racing was supported by the local landed gentry and members of the Caledonian Hunt. Ayr is regarded as the premier racecourse in Scotland.

During the First World War an airfield was established at Ayr racecourse. It was operational between September 1917 and September 1921.

I flew up to Glasgow International airport this morning then took a taxi to Paisley Gilmour Street station and met my friend Roland who I used to work with at British Airways, on the train. We walked to the track after we arrived at Ayr railway station and just made it to the racecourse in time for the first race.

The first two races both had very short priced favourites, Havana Grey at 4/7 in race 1 and Longroom at 1/4 in the second. Both horses won readily, Havana Grey by 5 lengths and Longroom by 3 ½ lengths. However as they were both so short, I decided not to back either of them, even in a win double, which would not quite have paid Even money (1.96/1).

I had my first bet of the day in the 3:00, run over 6 furlongs, the third consecutive sprint (the first two races were both run over 5 furlongs). My selection was Our Place in Loule, the 6/1 favourite in this 15 runner contest. He raced prominently and chased the clear winner over a furlong out, only losing second towards the finish. Duncan Of Scotland, an 11/1 chance made all and kept on well in the final furlong to beat Sea Of Green, who took second close home but had no chance with the winner.

Arnold, my selection in the fourth race was a well backed favourite, backed in from 2/1 to 13/8. He was slowly into his stride, held up and made no impression on the leading group, finishing fourth to Ching Ching Lor, which led well inside the final furlong and stayed on strongly to beat Hollywood Harry by half a length at the line.

My selection in the fifth race drifted like the proverbial barge in the betting from 7/1 to 12/1. He led until ridden and headed 3 furlongs out, finishing last of the six runners, 36 ¾ lengths behind Jonny Delta, the 5/2 favourite winner, and 10 lengths behind the fifth horse.

My selection in the 4:30, Kharbetation was unruly at the star, failed to enter the stalls and was withdrawn, the race going to Sophie P, which held on well close home to beat Nicholas T by a short head.

I rounded off the day by backing Kiwi Bay, an 8/1 chance in the last race. He took a keen hold and was close up until ridden and weakened well over a furlong out, finishing last of the seven runners, 13 ¾ lengths behind Testa Rossa the 10/1 winner.

Walked back to Ayr railway station immediately after the last race, caught 17:24 train to Paisley then bus to Glasgow Airport, arriving in plenty of time for my 20:30 flight to London Heathrow, unlike my trip to Perth last week which very nearly went pear shaped!

Wednesday 10th May - Newton Abbot

Today is my seventh visit to Newton Abbot races, my first in nine years, but my first midweek visit. All six of my previous trips here have been on Saturdays. A beautiful sunny and warm day today.

There are several sets of alms houses in Newton Abbot. The original Newton Abbot poorhouse was based in East Street, and the cellar of the Devon Arms was used as the oakum picking room, where paupers were given the unpleasant task of untwisting old rope top provide oakum, used to seal the seams of wooden boats.

An interesting fact about Newton Abbot is that it holds an annual Cheese and Onion Fayre in honour of Saint Leonard at the beginning of September every year.

Newton Abbot racecourse was the most westerly racecourse in Britain until Ffos Las racecourse opened in 2009.

My train from London took a rather circuitous route to Newton Abbot, via Bath and Bristol, which took nearly 3 ½ hours. However I still managed to walk to the racecourse and arrived in good time for the first race at 2:05pm. The roundabout just before the racecourse is called Balls corner, which my puerile mind found mildly amusing! Saw my friend Steve again today. He lives near Newton Abbot so that was not exactly a surprise!

I wasn't going to have a bet in the opener. The favourite, Brillare Momento (which I back at 10/1 20 days ago when it won its last race at Cheltenham) started at the prohibitive odds of 1/3. I did however decide in the end to have a small wager on Momella, which I managed to get at 9/1 (10.0) on Betfair. It went off the 5/1 third favourite. Pomme, the 3/1 second favourite led until it ran wide on the bend after the sixth flight of hurdles and was pulled up before the next obstacle. Momella led from that point onwards and quickened clear, hit the last but ran on strongly to readily beat Brillare Momento by 2 lengths, the pair 44 lengths clear of the third horse home. Had a pint of Tribute ale after the race to celebrate and slake my thirst.

Master Jake, my selection in the 3 1/4 mile chase, tracked the leaders but lost his action and was pulled up before the 13th fence. Southfield Vic, the 9/4 favourite led after the 16th and drew well clear from 3 out and won easily, beating Wadswick Court, which finished second by 24 lengths.

I was going to back Amour De Nuit in the third race, but it shortened from an opening 6/4 to start the 5/4 favourite. I had decided I was not going to back it unless I could get at least 2/1. That proved to be a wise decision, as although Amour De Nuit tracked the leaders and led 2 out it was headed at the last but could not hold off the late challenge of Talent To Amuse.

My selection in race 4, Fox Appeal, which I backed at just over 15/2 on Betfair (8.6) was backed in to 5/2 second favourite at the off. He raced keenly, tracked the leader and challenged 4 out and looked the likely winner before making a bad mistake at the second last and falling back to third. He rallied to grab second, but Henryville, the 3/1 winner had already flown by then and won by 5 lengths.

I backed Dites Rien, the 7/2 favourite in the fifth race. He raced in mid-division, was pushed along at the seventh where he was hampered. He did not have a clear run on the home bend but was switched out and made some ground to finish in third place, 15 ¼ lengths behind Clearly Capable the 6/1 lucky winner, who blundered badly at the last and Richard Johnson did well to stay on.

I did not have a bet in the sixth race as the favourite; Capitaine was long odds on (4/9). After jumping badly right at the first he recovered to track the leader, led after the third, was clear after the seventh and won easily by 10 lengths from The Gipper, the 15/8 second favourite. I rounded off the day with Muffins For Tea, the horse (not an afternoon snack). He started the 2/1 favourite having opened at 3/1. I managed to get 5/1 (6.0) on Betfair. He tracked the leader, led 2 out, made a mistake at the last but kept on well and won readily by 2 lengths.

Popped in to The Richard Hopkins, a Wetherspoons pub in Newton Abbot for a bite to eat and a pint. The premises were built in the 1850's and, like the adjacent Hopkins lane, takes its name from a local baker Richard Hopkins who once owned the land on which the pub stands, the family having been millers in the 18th century.

Thursday 12th May - Chester

Chester was founded as a "castrum" or Roman fort with the name Deva Victrix in the reign of Emperor Vespasian in 79 AD. It is one of the best preserved walled cities in Britain. The Saxons extended and strengthened the walls of Chester to protect the city against the Danes, who occupied it for short time until Alfred seized all the cattle and laid waste the surrounding land to drive them out. Apart from a 100 metre section, the Grade I listed walls are almost complete.

Today is my seventh visit to the historic racecourse of Chester and my first since 2011. Chester racecourse, otherwise known as the Roodee is according to official records the oldest racecourse still in use in England. Horse racing at Chester dates back to the early 16th century. It is also the smallest racecourse in England with a circumference of 1 mile and 1 furlong.

The racecourse lies on the banks of the River Dee and was once a harbour during the Roman settlement of the city. Towards the centre of the infield is a raised mound which is decorated by a small cross known as a "rood". It is from this that the racecourse derives the name "Roodee", which is a corruption of "Rood Eye", meaning "The Island of the Cross".

According to legend the cross marks the burial site of a statue of the Virgin Mary sentenced to hang after causing the death of Lady Trawst. The legend states that she had gone to church to pray for rain but when her prayers were answered by a tremendous thunderstorm the statue was dislodged and fell, killing her. As a holy object, hanging or burning the statue would be sacrilege so the statue was left by the banks of the river and the tide carried it down to Chester. The statue was found guilty by a jury of 12 men. If the legend is true, then this was the first recorded case of a jury being used in court.

Back to the 21st Century! I took a train from Euston and arrived at Chester railway station just before 1:30pm, giving me just enough time to walk to the track to see the first race. Another beautiful, sunny and warm day. Fortunately today was a reciprocal day at Chester on my York badge, as admission to the County Stand today was £52!

I had considered backing Khairaat, the 10/11 favourite in the first race, with Dahik, the 4/6 favourite in the fifth race, but decided against it in the end. Khairaat duly obliged, making all in the opener and drawing clear, winning comfortably by 4 ½ lengths.

I backed Poet's Word in the second race. It raced in touch, went second inside the final furlong, ran on and closed near the finish but was always held, beaten a neck by Deauville, the 6/4 favourite.

My selection in the third race was Mutawatheb, which started as one of the 7/2 joint favourites, however I got 5/1 (6.0) on Betfair. It raced in touch, improved to go second just over a furlong out, led 150 yards out and was in control at the finish, beating Masham Star by 1 ¼ lengths.

I backed Tamleek in the fourth raced. It was held up in touch, chased the leaders over a furlong out but was one paced in the final 150 yards, going down by 2 ¼ lengths, finishing fourth to Venice Beach the 5/2 favourite.

I did not have a bet in the fifth race. The horse which I was originally planning to back, Dahik, in a double with the first race winner, came a disappointing fourth, six lengths behind Dragons Tail.

Although I had had a bet in the sixth race on Munro, an 11/1 chance I decided to leave before the race, in order to grab a bite to eat and a pint in the local Wetherspoons pub en-route to the station before my train home. Munro apparently ran a blinder, running on when he did not get a clear run, hampered in the final furlong and finished strongly, only going down by a neck to Zamjar the 11/4 favourite.

Wednesday 17th May - York

York was founded by the Romans as Eboracum in 71 AD. It became the capital of the Roman province of Britannia Inferior, and later of the kingdoms of Deira, Northumbria and Jorvik. The Emperors Hadrian, Septimus Severus and Constantius I all held court in York during their various campaigns.

In 1068, two years after the Norman conquest of England, the people of York rebelled. Initially they were successful, but upon the arrival of William the Conqueror the rebellion was put down. In

1190, York Castle was the site of an infamous massacre of its Jewish inhabitants, in which at least 150 Jews died (although some authorities put the figure as high as 500).

York was voted European Tourism City of the Year by European Cities Marketing in June 2007, beating 130 other European cities to gain first place, surpassing Gothenburg in Sweden (second) and Valencia in Spain (third). York was also voted the safest place to visit in the 2010 Conde Nast Traveller Readers' Choice Awards. In 2018 The Sunday Times deemed York to be its overall 'Best Place to Live' in Britain. The result was confirmed in a YouGov survey, reported in August 2018, with 92% of respondents saying that they liked the city, more than any of 56 other British cities.

A damp, dreary and rainy day today. My racing mate and friend from my schooldays, Keith came racing with me to York today. After arriving at York railway station we walked down Nunnery Lane to The Trafalgar Bay public house, met up with three other friends, Denis, Chris and Owen and enjoyed two excellent pints of John Smiths' Old Brewery Bitter before walking to the track.

The going today was Good to Soft due to significant rainfall. It was Good to Firm earlier in the week.

I selected Lovell, the Charlie Appleby trained, Godolphin owned 6/1 favourite in the first race. He tracked the leading duo until pushed along over 3 furlongs out before weakening and finishing last of the 20 runners, 37 ¾ lengths behind Master Carpenter, the 12/1 winner, which made smooth headway and stayed on strongly to beat Al Neksh by 5 lengths.

In race 2 I chose Muntadab. He led narrowly, was ridden over a furlong out, kept on but was headed close home, beaten a neck by the 25/1 winner, Al Qahwa.

My selection in the third race was The Tin Man. He chased the leaders , made headway 2 furlongs out, was ridden over a furlong out before gradually weakening, finishing in fifth place, 6 ¼ lengths adrift from Tasleet, the 14/1 Hamdan Al Maktoum easy winner.

I took a chance with Vintage Folly, a 12/1 chance against Shutter Speed the 4/7 favourite. Vintage Folly tracked the leader making good headway and was close up 3 furlongs out. He chased the winner 2 furlongs out, was driven and kept on in the final furlong. Shutter Speed, the Khalid Abdullah owned, John Gosden trained and Frankie Dettori ridden favourite kept on to win by a length and three quarters.

I backed Starlight Romance in the fifth race. She tracked the leaders, was ridden to challenge a furlong out and kept on, finishing third to Battered, the 4/1 favourite.

Keith and I needed to leave before the seventh race in order to catch our booked train home so the 5:05 race was our last. My selection was Savalas, which raced prominently and held every chance over a furlong out before keeping on at the same pace in the final furlong, going down by 3 ¼ lengths and finishing fifth to Santry the 9/4 favourite.

For the record Zain Arion, a 20/1 shot won the seventh race, beating Purple Rock a 14/1 chance by a length and a half.

I am going racing at York again for the next two days and Newbury on Friday before resuming my racecourse tour at Market Rasen on Sunday.

Sunday 21st May - Market Rasen

The place-name 'Market Rasen' is first attested in the Domesday Book of 1086, where it appears as Rase, Rasa and Resne. The name derives from the Old English raesn meaning 'plank', and is thought to refer to a plank bridge. The River Rase runs through the town from East to West. The town is known for Market Rasen Racecourse and being close to the epicentre of a 2008 earthquake! On 27 February 2008 a significant earthquake had its epicentre approximately 2.5 miles north-west of Market Rasen, near the neighbouring parish of Middle Rasen.

The earthquake, which measured 5.2 on the Richter Sclae , struck at a depth of 11.6 miles and was felt across much of the UK from Edinburgh to Plymouth, and as far away as Bangor in Northern Ireland and Haarlem in the Netherlands. The 10-second quake was the largest recorded example in the United Kingdom since the 1984 Llyn Peninsula earthquake, measuring 5.4 struck North Wales. There were no recorded local injuries and only one recorded injury elsewhere in the UK, in South Yorkshire, when a chimney was dislodged from a house, falling down though the house's roof and landing on the male resident, who was in bed at the time, causing a broken pelvis.

Today is only my third visit to Market Rasen (colloquially referred to as Market Raspberry for some unknown reason) races. I travelled here by train today, which is something of a minor miracle as there are only three trains a day on Sundays!

On picking up a racecard on arrival I noticed that the Chairman of Market Rasen racecourse is called Tommy Cooper. Just like that! I don't suppose he wears a fez or does magic tricks, but who knows? It could be his party piece.

I walked the mile or so from Market Rasen railway station to the racecourse and arrived about an hour before the first race. I did not have a bet in the opener as the favourite was unbackable at the prohibitive odds of 1/7 and duly won like a good thing by 8 lengths.

In the 2:20 race Too Many Diamonds was going for a fourth win in eight days. He won the 3:05 at Bangor-on-Dee the previous day. Although I fancied his chance, I could not bring myself to back him at 8/11. I do not generally like backing any horse to win in a single bet at less than Even money. I decided to have a small saver on Jupiter Custos at 12/1. He ran quite well, eventually finishing third and only losing second place near the finish. Too Many Diamonds won, completing a remarkable training and riding feat for Dan and Harry Skelton (the trainer and jockey).

I was going to back Always Lion in the third race but only if I could get 2/1 or better. Always Lion went off at 7/4 and won. C'est la vie!

I backed Viserion in the fourth race, a 2 ½ mile hurdle with 15 runners. He chased the leaders, made a mistake at the fourth flight of fences, was given a reminder but then lost place and gradually weakened before being pulled up before 2 out. Sandymount, a 16/1 shot won the race.

Yorkist carried my money in the fifth event, a 2 mile 3 furlongs chase. He raced prominently, chasing the leader until ridden and weakening when left third when Baby King fell when going well.

I'dliketheoption, one of the 3/1 co-favourites ran on well to claim the prize by 3 ½ lengths from Voix D'Eau.

I saddled Ultimatum Du Roy with my selection in the sixth race. He chased the leader to the fourth fence and remained handy until losing his place at the tenth. He rallied to go second shortly after and had every chance 2 out but could find no extra on the flat and finished third to Emerald Rose, beaten by just over 5 lengths.

I backed Brecon Hill at 2/1 in the bumper, before the withdrawal of Quick Pick, the favourite. Brecon Hill won the race however I was hit by a hefty Rule 4 deduction.

I had a wait of around an hour and a half in Market Rasen before by return train in which time I noticed that lots of shops in the town centre were flying the Lincolnshire flag. Prior to today I did not know that Lincolnshire had a flag! I also noticed a curious road sign pointing to a place called Mamers 385 miles (620 kilometres) away! Apparently, Market Rasen is twinned with Mamers. I have never seen the point and still cannot see the point of twinning towns.

Monday 22nd May - Carlisle

Today is only my fifth day's racing at Carlisle. My last visit was 7 years ago.

The early history of Carlisle was as a Roman settlement, established to serve the forts on Hadrian's Wall. During the Middle Ages, Carlisle became an important military stronghold due to its proximity to the Kingdom of Scotland. By the time of the Norman Conquest in 1066, Carlisle was part of Scotland, This changed in 1092, when William The Conqueror's son Rufus invaded the region and incorporated Cumberland and Carlisle into England.

The conquest of Cumberland was the beginning of a war between Scotland and England which saw the region around Carlisle change hands a number of times. During the wars, the livelihood of people on the border (known as Border Reivers) was devastated by armies from both sides. Even when the countries were not at war tension remained high.

The Reivers became so much of a nuisance to the Scottish and English governments that, in 1525, the Archbishop of Glasgow Gavin Dunbar cursed all the reivers of the borderlands. The curse was detailed in 1,069 words, beginning "I curse their head and all the hairs on their head; I curse their face, their brain (innermost thoughts), their mouth, their nose, their tongue, their teeth, their teeth, their forehead, their shoulders, their breast, their heart, their stomach, their back, their womb, their arms, their legs, their hands, their feet and every part of their body, from the top of their head to the soles of their feet, before and behind, within and without."

That was them well and truly told!

I arrived at Carlisle railway station around 12:45 and walked the 2.3 miles to the racecourse. Before the first race I met Pat, a very good friend of mine who moved up to Cumbria around 15 years ago, and is now in his 80th year.

I selected Ventura Dragon in the opening 5 furlong sprint and had requested minimum odds of 2/1 (3.0) on Betfair. He went off at 5/4 so I assumed that I was not on. Ventura Dragon and Seyaady fought out the finish with magic mark in close pursuit. To the surprise of nearly everyone on the racecourse, including the cameraman who zoomed in on Seyaady after the finish, Ventura Dragon won the race on the nod by a nose (or the length of a gnat's dick as a good friend of mine has said in the past). To my delight I found out that my bet had been taken so I had unknowingly backed the winner.

Mr Orange carried my money in the second event, a six furlong sprint. He led after 2 furlongs and was close up 2 furlongs out but was outpace inside the final furlong, finishing fourth and beaten 3 ½ lengths behind Merdon Castle.

I fancied Ravenhoe in the mile race. He was held up, ridden over 2 furlongs out and made no impression in the final furlong and finished eighth of the eleven runners, 5 ¾ lengths behind Pensax Boy, the 16/1 winner. My friend Pat backed the winner.

I narrowed the fourth race down to two. Heir Of Excitement and Il Sicario. I chose Il Sicario. He tracked the leaders, made an effort 2 furlongs out but weakened inside the final furlong and finished fifth. Needless to say Heir Of Excitement won the race, prevailing in a tight finish. The first four come could have been covered by a large horse blanket. The winning distances between the first four home were only a neck, short head and a neck.

I decided to make the 4:20 my last race of the day. I backed Four Wishes. He tracked the leaders, was driven along 2 furlongs out but could make no impression on the leading trio inside the final furlong and finished fourth, a length and three quarters behind Right Action, the 4/1 favourite.

I then walked back to Carlisle station to catch my train back to London at 17:53. I had forgotten until I looked at my train ticket that I had booked back in First Class so that was a nice end to the day.

The following day I received a lovely email from Pat saying it was good to see me and that I must have brought him luck as he had four winners. Good on him.

Tuesday 23rd May - Brighton

My seventh consecutive day's racing today and my 47th UK racecourse visited this year.

Brighton's location has made it a popular destination for tourists. It is the most popular UK seaside destination for overseas tourists. Renowned for its diverse communities, quirky shopping areas, large cultural, music and arts scene and its large LGBT population, Brighton is recognised as the "unofficial gay capital of the UK". Brighton has been called the UK's "hippest city", and along with Norwich, named as one of the UK's most 'Godless' cities, and "the happiest place to live in the UK".

In 2011, as part of the Jedi census phenomenon, 2.6% of Brighton residents claimed their religion was Jedi Knight, the largest percentage in the country.

Brighton racecourse was immortalised in the Graham Greene novel and 1948 film 'Brighton Rock', a murder thriller set in 1930's Brighton.

My train from London arrived at Brighton at 1:30pm. The first race at Brighton was at 2;20. There is usually a courtesy bus waiting to take punters to the racecourse but I think the last one had gone so I walked up the steep hill instead, arriving at the course around 2:05. A good, albeit unplanned, cardio-vascular workout for me!

I backed Fusion Central in the opener, opposing Arabian Jazz the drifting favourite. My fancy was slow into its stride and never really got into the race, finishing eighth of the ten runners, 5 ½ lengths behind Holdenhurst the 12/1 winner.

My fancy in the second race was Pass The Cristal. He was held up towards the rear, was ridden and made headway approaching the final furlong and was driven out to win by a neck.

Before the third race I saw Alan, a professional acquaintance of mine. As it happened, he had a horse running, Staintondale Lass, the 3/1 outsider running in the race. I had previously decided that I would not have a bet in the race. I was not convinced that Black Bess, the 11/10 favourite would win but I did not fancy either of the other two runners. I was correct insofar as Black Bess was beaten, albeit only by a neck by Staintondale Lass. At the presentation ceremony Alan said that he his favourite racecourse was Lingfield as he had had the winner of the Winter Derby there and was known as the Lord Of Lingfield, any jokingly said he should now also be known as the Baron of Brighton.

I was distracted before the fourth race and did not manage to get my intended bet on Deep Challenger on before the off. That proved to be a lucky happenstance as although Deep Challenger led approaching the final furlong he was then headed and kept on one pace and finished second, beaten 4 lengths by Impressive Day, a 25/1 outsider.

I backed Provoking in the 4:20 race which ran keenly in mid-division before being ridden 2 furlongs out and never got on terms, finishing seventh of the fourteen runners, nearly ten lengths behind Master Of Heaven, the 10/1 winner, which made all and just held of the late challenge of Tommys Geal by a short head.

Sheer Intensity provided me with my second winner of the afternoon in the sixth race. She was held up, made headway over a furlong out, led in the final ½ furlong and ran on well, winning by 1 ¾ lengths.

A sea mist had begun to descend by the seventh race, reducing visibility significantly. I backed Buzz Lightyere, the 11/8 favourite in the race. He chased the leaders, keeping on in close third, but took a hefty bump inside the final furlong, kept on but did not have time to recover before the post came. Suitsus, a 16/1 chance took the race by 2 lengths from With Approval, with Buzz Lightyere a further 1 ¼ lengths behind in third.

By the time of the eighth race the sea mist had descended even further. My selection, Duke Of North, the 9/4 favourite tracked the leaders, but had already weakened into sixth when the field came back into view and finished sixth of the seven runners. Perfect Pastime, a 16/1 shot took the race.

I am planning to do a 'double header' at Goodwood on Thursday afternoon and Sandown Park in the evening on Thursday and York on Saturday before resuming my racecourse tour at Beverley next Wednesday.

Wednesday 31st May - Beverley

Today is only my fourth visit to Beverley races. Summer hopefully is not too far away now. A lovely glorious sunny and warm day today at Beverley.

Horse racing has a long history in Beverley, with evidence of a permanent race track reaching as far back as 1690, with its first grandstand was built in 1767. As well as its racecourse and markets, Beverley is known for hosting various food and music festivals throughout the year. The town was listed in the 2018 Sunday Times report on Best Places to Live in Northern England.

My train from King's Cross to Doncaster was slightly delayed due to a slow running train ahead of it. As a result I missed my connection and had to wait an hour for the next one. So, instead of arriving at Beverley racecourse an hour before the first race I got there with only five minutes to spare.

My selection in the first of the three five furlong sprints on the card was Our Little Pony, which just failed to get to Popsi by a short head in their previous encounter at Redcar on 4th May. Today they met again and Popsi had a two pound pull at the weights. Pops raced close up and was ridden to take the lead just over a furlong from home. Our Little Pony tracked her and did not have a clear run so had to switch just over a furlong out. She was soon ridden to challenge and stayed on to lead and was a length and a quarter up at the winning post. A good start to the day!

In the second event I backed The Armed Man. He raced wide, chased the leaders making headway two furlongs out. However Jacob's Pillow led approaching the final furlong and he could make no impression on him and went down by a length.

In the 3:00 race, the third of the 5 furlong sprints on the card I backed Dundunah, the 11/4 joint favourite. She tracked the leaders and switched left and was making headway when hampered just over a furlong out. She stayed on to challenge in the last 100 yards but could find no extra near the finish, going down by half a length to Crosse Fire, which was driven to lead in the final 75 yards.

My selection in the 3:30 was Wink Oliver, which won the 3:00 at Redcar yesterday. He dwelt leaving the stalls and raced towards the rear, made some headway two furlongs out, was ridden a furlong out, keeping on and was nearest at the line, finishing seventh to Talent Scout.

My selection in the fifth race was Palmerston, the 5/2 favourite. He tracked the leading pair, made headway 2 furlongs out and was ridden to lead entering the final furlong. He was soon joined and driven and kept on well towards the finish and won by ¾ of a length from Haraz.

I chose Monsieur Glory, the 9/4 favourite in the sixth race. He was held up in touch, and made some headway over a furlong out. He made some effort shortly after, when hampered entering the final furlong and was soon ridden. He stayed on well towards the finish, but could not get to Bromance, a 12/1 shot, finishing fourth to him.

I fancied Time's Arrow, the 4/11 favourite in the seventh race, which was too short for me to contemplate backing so I left the racecourse in search of a pub for a quick pint before my train home. As it happened Time's Arrow just failed by a nose.

Next stop Hexham on Saturday.

Saturday 3rd June - Hexham

Like many towns in the Anglo-Scottish border area, Hexham suffered from the border wars between the kingdoms of England and Scotland, including attacks from William Wallace who burnt the town in 1297. In 1312, Robert the Bruce, King of Scotland, demanded and received £2,000 from the town and monastery in order for them to be spared a similar fate. In 1346 the monastery was sacked in a later invasion by King David II of Scotland.

In 1761, the Hexham Riot took place in the Market Place when a crowd protesting about changes in the criteria for serving in the militia was fired upon by troops from the North Yorkshire Militia, earning the Militia the sobriquet of The Hexham Butchers.

The Old Gaol in Hexham was one of the first purpose-built jails in England. It was built between 1330 and 1333 and is a Grade I listed Scheduled Monument.

A long day today. I left home at 07:00 this morning in order to catch the 08:30 train from King's Cross to Newcastle and connecting train to Hexham. Today is my sixth visit to Hexham racecourse, which promotes itself, quite rightly in my opinion, as the most picturesque racecourse in the country.

On arrival at Hexham railway station I walked into the town and saw a queue of people by the bus station. Most of them were going to the racecourse, which is over 2 miles away up a steep hill, so as taxis arrived, groups of us got in them to take us to the racecourse for the piffling sum of £1 each.

One of the guys in my taxi very kindly gave me a voucher for reduced admission at a number of northern racecourses, including Hexham and Thirsk (where I am going on Monday). I decided to take advantage of the £10 Grandstand pensioners' admission today and save the voucher for Thirsk on Monday.

It was a glorious sunny and warm day at Hexham. The racecard was only £2 which is a rarity these days. Most are £3 or more and a lot are £5 on big race days.

In the first race, a 2 mile hurdle, I backed Back To Balloo, which won by 20 lengths at Fakenham in its previous run on 9th May over the same trip. He tracked the leaders and led approaching 2 out. However Towering, the 5/2 second favourite stalked his every move and led approaching the last and was driven out to win by just under 2 lengths.

I was going to back City Dreamer, the short priced favourite in the second race, but only if I could get Even Money. He went off the ½ favourite having touched 4/9, tracked the leaders and was upsides at the last but could only finish second to Costa Percy, an 8/1 chance, which led approaching the last and was driven right out to win by a length.

I backed Hattons Hill in the third event which was attempting to win his fifth race on the bounce at Hexham. He raced prominently throughout and stayed on strongly in the last 100 yards to head Lilly's Legend, in the final stride by a short head. Lilly's Legend was a slightly unlucky loser as he spread a right hind shoe, which may have cost him the race.

I backed Beyondtemptation in the fourth race. He led until after the fourth and was in second position when he fell at the next, the race going to Desert Island Dusk, the 9/4 favourite, who led after the fourth and stayed on well approaching the last to win by just over 3 lengths.

I had a 45 minute walk to look forward to get to Hexham station in time for my train at 5:22, so the last race I could stay for was the 3:50. I backed Miss Conway, the 7/2 favourite. She led until before the 12th, then lost her place a bit before rallying to chase the leader between the last two. She kept on but could make no impression on Dica, a 22/1 outsider which stayed on strongly to win by 4 ½ lengths.

I reached Ladbrokes in Hexham at 4:35 about 10 seconds before the start of The Epsom Derby, which was won by Wings Of Eagles, a 40/1 outsider. I did not have a bet in race.

My train from Newcastle to London was delayed by 33 minutes due to a trespasser, on the main line, so we were diverted before re-joining the main line further down, and arrived at King's Cross at 22:15. At least I should get a few quid back from Virgin Trains under their Delay Repay scheme.

Monday 5th June - Thirsk

Archaeological finds indicate that there was a settlement at Thirsk around 500-600 BC. Thirsk is built around a large medieval market square, which still hosts an open-air market on Mondays and Saturdays.

Thirsk was home to veterinary surgeon and author James Herriot. He called Thirsk Darrowby in his semi-autobiographical books about a vet's life in the Yorkshire Dales.

The present racecourse at Thirsk opened in 1923, however racing had taken place on the old course over 200 years earlier.

Today is my eighth visit to Thirsk races and number Fifty on my racecourse tour. A generally wet and miserable day although the sun did make an attempt to break through once or twice during the afternoon in between torrential downpours!

Took the 09:08 Virgin Train from King's Cross to York, arriving there at 11:50, around 20 minutes late due to a slow and late running train in front. Decided to pop into The Trafalgar Bay pub in Nunnery Lane in York for a pint of their excellently kept John Smith's Old Brewery Bitter, which at the time of writing is only £2 a pint!

Caught the 13:15 TransPennine Express train to Thirsk, which arrived on schedule at 13:31. A courtesy bus to the racecourse then took racegoers the short distance to Thirsk racecourse.

My selection in the first of four 6 furlong sprints on the card was Mabo. He was predicted to be the 5/4 favourite in the Racing Post, opened at 2/1 on course and drifted out to 3/1 at the off. An ominous sign! Mabo tracked the leaders before being pushed along 2 furlongs out and making no impression and finishing in seventh position, 7 ¾ lengths behind the inappropriately named Another Day of Sun, the 5/6 favourite.

My intended selection, Rampant Lion, in the second race was withdrawn shortly before the 'off' so I ended up not having a bet in the race, which was won by Jedi Master the 8/15 favourite which quickened well and won easily.

I chose My Renaissance to carry my money in the 3:00 race. He tracked Tonto's Spirit, the 5/2 favourite and eventual winner, before being ridden well over a furlong out and weakening into sixth, 9 ¾ lengths behind him.

I backed Meshardal in the 3:30. He was held up on the outer, tracking the leaders over 2 furlongs out. He was still 4 lengths behind with only a furlong to go but stayed on really well to lead near the post, winning by a neck from Round The Island, a 25/1 outsider.

The heavens opened before the fifth race so I decided to watch it from the comfort of the bar area. My selection, Kenstone, ridden by Hollie Doyle, started at 15/2 however I had secured 10/1 (11.0) on Betfair earlier in the day. He raced in touch making smooth headway 3 furlongs out, led well over a furlong out and won by a country mile. The official winning distance was 10 lengths.

I backed Stubytuesday in the sixth race. He chased the leaders until being ridden and making no impression from 2 furlongs out and finished ninth, 10 ¼ lengths behind Uncle Charlie, the 10/1 winner.

White Rosa was my selection in the 5:05. She raced in touch, made headway 3 furlongs out, had to switch 1 ½ furlongs out when not much room, was driven inside the final furlong and kept on well but could not get to Lyric Harmony, the 7/4 favourite who prevailed by ¾ of a length.

I gave the 5:35 race a miss to give me good time to get to the station in time to catch my train back to York. On arrival at York I had time for another quick trip to The Trafalgar Bay before returning to the station for my train back to London.

Wednesday 7th June - Hamilton

The town of Hamilton was originally known as Cadzow or Cadyou. During the Wars of Scottish Independence the Hamilton family initially supported the English and Walter Fitz Gilbert (the head of the Hamilton family) was governor of Bothwell Castle on behalf of the English. However, following the Battle of Bannockburn, he later changed his loyalty to Robert the Bruce, and ceded Bothwell to him. For this act, he was rewarded with a portion of land which had been forfeited by the Comyns at Dalserf and later the Barony and lands of Cadzow. Cadzow was renamed Hamilton in the time of James, Lord Hamilton, who was married to Princess Mary, the daughter of King James II.

Today is my fifth visit to Hamilton Park races, Number 51 on my racecourse tour and 75th race meeting of 2017. I did not realise until I was en-route to Heathrow Airport this morning that there was a 7 am inspection. There had been 39mm of rain at Hamilton (1 ½ inches in old money) since Saturday as at 3:30pm yesterday, with more rain forecast. Fortunately that did not materialise and the meeting went ahead on what turned out in the end to be a glorious afternoon weather-wise. There were however 25 non-runners due to the change of going.

I purchased a One Day bus ticket on arrival at Glasgow airport, took the airport express into Buchanan Street then a #255 bus which dropped me right outside the racecourse about half an hour before the first race. Perfect!

My selection in the opening 6 furlong sprint was 5 furlong sprint was Lina's Star, the 2/1 second favourite. She pressed the leader until ridden over a furlong out, weakened in the final half furlong and finished last of the four runners, 6 lengths behind Miss bar Beach, the 11/8 favourite.

I backed Don Valentino, which just started favourite at 11/8, in the second race, another 6 furlong sprint. He tracked the leaders, raced keenly and joined the leader just over a furlong out. He was then driven but could find no extra towards the finish and came second, half a length behind Souls In The Wind, the 6/4 second favourite.

I was going to back High Expectations in the third race, provided I could get at least 6/4 about it. He started at 11/10 so I did not have a bet. That proved fortunate as, although he chased the leader and actually led 3 furlongs out, he was headed just over a furlong out and weakened badly into third at the line, 9 ¼ lengths behind Mistiness, the 15/8 winner.

A similar story in race four. I wanted to back Amy Blair if I could get Evens about it. He opened at 4/6 and went off the 4/5 favourite, so once again I did not have a bet in the race. He led until ridden 2 furlongs out, was headed over a furlong out and weakened inside the final furlong, finishing fourth of the six runners, 4 ¾ lengths behind Dark Crystal, the 15/2 winner, which was ridden clear inside the final furlong, was pushed out towards the finish and won by 2 ¼ lengths.

Gulf Of Poets carried my money in the 4:10 race. He tracked the leaders and led going well over 2 furlongs out, edged left entering the final furlong , kept on well and was eased towards the finish, winning by a comfortable 1 ¼ lengths.

I backed Royal Connoisseur in the sixth event, another 6 furlong sprint. He chased the leader, was ridden over 2 furlongs out, weakened in the final furlong and finished last of the five runners, 7 ¼ lengths behind Inexes, the 3/1 winner.

I backed Roy's Legacy, the previous year's winner in the closing 5 furlong race. He raced prominently, was ridden 2 furlongs out before weakening into fourth, 5 ¾ lengths behind Kinglami, the 4/1 winner.

A short non-racing break for Keith and me in Madeira for the next few days, before I resume the racecourse tour at Yarmouth next Tuesday.

Tuesday 13th June - Yarmouth

Number 52 on the racecourse tour today. Down to single digits to go now! Today is my fourth visit to Great Yarmouth races and my first in 16 years.

An interesting fact about Great Yarmouth is that nearly 200 years ago it suffered the greatest single loss of life in a bridge disaster. On Friday 2nd May 1845 hundreds of men, women and children lined the river and crowded onto the Suspension Bridge waiting to see a free circus spectacle. Nelson the clown, sitting in a washtub was to be pulled up the river by four white geese with scarlet ribbons for reins.

More than 500 people crammed onto the Suspension Bridge to get the best view. As they strained and shifted to catch the first glimpse of the geese, the bridge chains snapped under their weight and they plunged into the river. 78 people lost their lives that day, including 59 children. To this day, the bridge disaster remains the greatest single loss of life in Great Yarmouth.

Back to the 21st Century. I was planning to back Tivoli, the favourite, to be ridden by Frankie Dettori in the first race, but only if I could get 2/1 on it. It was trading at around 5/4 when it unshipped Frankie in the paddock and was withdrawn, and Frankie was stood down for the day by the course doctor, having been slightly injured. In the end I did not have a bet in the race, which was won by Hermosita, the new 9/4 favourite.

In the second race, a 5 runner event, I backed Falak at 3/1 and had a small saver on St Andrews at 11/1. They came 3rd and 4th respectively, the race going to Hawkerland the 5/6 favourite, who got up in the dying strides to deny Bostonian in the third event, in what turned out to be a three horse race due to Poppy Time being a non-runner. As is often the case in three horse races, Theydon Girls the 10/11 favourite was beaten, however on this occasion the outsider of three did not win. Ms Gillard led in the final 50 yards to deny my selection by a neck. Theydon Girls finished a poor third, a further 10 lengths behind.

I backed Favorite Girl, the 7/2 outsider in what turned out to be a three horse race in the 3:15. As is often the case in such races the favourite, Theydon Girls was beaten. My selection ran well and led a furlong out, only to be headed by Ms Gillard in the final 50 yards. Theydon Girls finished a poor third, 10 lengths behind.

I backed Moolazim in the fourth race. He took a keen hold, was held up in touch in midfield, quickened to lead over a furlong out and ran on strongly to win readily by 2 ½ lengths.

Ocean Temptress, the 11/4 favourite carried my money in the fifth race. She was held up in touch in midfield, was ridden and chased the leaders over a furlong out but had no chance with the winner, Patching, inside the final furlong, but kept on to go second towards the finish.

I backed both African Trader and Tigersin in the sixth race. They finished in sixth and eighth place respectively behind Himalayan Queen.

As I had a train to catch, I missed the last race.

Next stop on the racecourse tour Worcester tomorrow, on what promises to be another lovely day weather-wise.

Wednesday 14th June - Worcester

The most famous landmark in Worcester is the imposing Anglican Worcester Cathedral. The current building, officially named the Cathedral Church of Christ and the Blessed Virgin Mary, was known as Worcester Priory before the English Reformation. Construction began in 1084. Its crypt dates back to the 10th century. The cathedral has the distinction of housing the tomb of King John.

The city of Worcester is known as the home of Royal Worcester Porcelain, composer Edward Elgar, Lea & Perrins, makers of traditional Worcestershire Sauce and Berrow's Worcester Journal, claimed to be the world's oldest newspaper.

The Battle of Worcester in 1651 was the final battle of the English Civil War, where Oliver Cromwell's New Model Army defeated King Charles II's Royalists.

A glorious and hot day today as predicted. Today is my seventh visit to Worcester races. I came here twice in 2015, the first occasion of which was 1st July, the first day of my retirement and the hottest day of the year! Before that my most recent previous visit was in 2001.

I had over an hour to kill after my train arrived in Worcester so I took the opportunity to visit The Crown (a JD Wetherspoon pub) and sample a couple of excellent pints of local cider before heading to the racecourse.

Worcester, like Perth in Scotland is unusual insofar as they are both jumps racecourses that only race in the summer. In the case of Perth it is due to the fact that it is located in the Scottish highlands. As far as Worcester is concerned the problem used to be due to the racecourse being frequently flooded in the winter months by the nearby river Severn.

I saw two friends at the races today, Steve, who lives near Newton Abbot and Maurice, who lives near Salisbury and is coming racing to Perth with Keith and me in September.

Racing commenced at 2:20 today. I plumped for Desertmore Hill, the 2/1 favourite in the opening 2 mile chase. He was held up, made headway four out, made a slight mistake at the next, led at the next and was ridden out to win by 2 ½ lengths. A good start to the day!

My selection in the second race, and final chase of the day was Mahlers Star. He chased the leaders, was ridden three approaching three out and stayed on one pace from then on, finishing in fifth spot, 8 ½ lengths behind Get Involved, the 16/1 winner.

Madam Anna carried my money in the bumper. She was held up, pushed along three furlongs out and weakened in the last quarter mile, and finished fifth, beaten nearly 20 lengths by Drumlynn, who stayed on well to beat Captiva Island, the 2/1 favourite by two lengths.

The remaining races were all hurdles. In the 3:20 I backed Lake Chapala. He was held up, made headway approaching three out, made a mistake at the last and could find no extra towards the finish and came fourth, beaten a length and a half, behind Jigsaw Financial, who led after the fifth and was driven out to beat Sir Dylan, a 33/1 shot, by a neck.

I backed Three Star General, a 13/8 chance against Burrows Lane, the 4/5 favourite. The two of them were well clear of the rest of the field turning for home. Burrows Lane took over the lead from

Three Star General before two out, went 5 lengths clear and looked the likely winner. However Three Star General switched to the stands rail and rallied really well on the flat to deny him by 4 ½ lengths at the line. The third horse, Ballyandrew, was a distant 46 lengths back.

The 4:50 was my last race of the day as I had a train to catch just before 5:30. I backed Deebaj, who was held up, made headway at the seventh flight and was ridden approaching the last, stayed on one pace on the flat until going second close home, but never threatening Ascendant, who won by 5 lengths.

I am going racing at Newbury tomorrow, York on Friday and Saturday and Royal Ascot on Tuesday, before resuming the racecourse tour at Ripon next Thursday.

Thursday 22nd June - Ripon

Day 54 on the racecourse tour and my eighth visit to Ripon racecourse.

Took the train to York and rented a car today. Drove near a couple more unusually named villages. Long Marston and Tockwith.

A few little known facts about Ripon. The city is noted for its main feature, Ripon Cathedral, which is architecturally significant. The city was originally known as Inhrypum and was founded by Saint Wilfrid during the time of the Anglian kingdom, a period in which it enjoyed prominence in terms of religious importance in Great Britain. It is also the third smallest city in England. According to the 2011 Census it had a population of 16,702. As well as its racecourse and cathedral, Ripon is a tourist destination because of its close proximity to the UNESCO World Heritage Site which consists of the Studly Royal Park and Fountains Abbey. The city itself is over 1,300 years old.

I arrived at the racecourse about an hour before the first race, a six furlong sprint, my selection in which was Noah Amor, which I decided to take a punt on, opposing Tatlisu, the 8/11 favourite. Noah Amor led after a furlong, was ridden 2 furlongs out and headed a furlong from home, weakening into 5th of the 6 runners, 5 ¾ lengths behind Tatlisu, which was held up, made smooth headway over two furlongs out and led going well over a furlong out.

In the 2:45, another 6 furlong sprint I backed Collingham Park, the 11/10 favourite, which I got nearly 9/4 on Betfair (3.2). He raced in touch, was soon ridden 2 furlongs out, was soon headed, kept on but was always held by the 7/1 winner, Mr Wagyu who kept on well and won by ¾ of a length.

My pick in the 3:20, the shortest race of the day, was Oriental Splendour. He raced midfield, was ridden over 2 furlongs out and weakened inside the final furlong, finishing sixth, 4 ¾ lengths behind Tarboosh, a 12/1 chance.

Phoenix Dawn carried my money in the mile and a half race. He led until ridden 2 furlongs out, and weakened over a furlong out to finish third, over 10 lengths behind Kilowatt, the 6/5 favourite.

Sands Chorus, the 5/2 favourite was my selection in the 4:25 race. He raced prominently and was ridden to lead over 2 furlongs out, was headed just over a furlong from the line and kept on at the same pace, finishing fourth, 1 ½ lengths adrift from Magic City at 9/1.

The 5:10 race was my last race of the day to ensure I would catch my booked return train. Presenting Julio, the 7/4 favourite and my last chance of finding a winner on the day, did a good impression of the horse in the old Hamlet cigar advert and virtually refused to race, giving away 25 lengths at the star! He raced well behind throughout and stood no chance. I left the racecourse while the race was still in progress.

On arrival back at York I managed to fit in a pint of Sam Smith's Old Brewery Bitter at the Trafalgar Bay pub, before catching my train home.

Thursday 29th June - Newmarket (July Course)

I am well into the home straight now. Only 6 more tracks to go on the racecourse tour.

Most of the Newmarket-based racing stables are situated in the centre of the town, where they can easily reach the gallops. The town has special horse routes so the horses can reach the gallops safely from the many training establishments occupied by top trainers. Many of the world's most successful trainers are based in Newmarket, Sir Michael Stoute, John Gosden, Saaed bin Suroor and Charlie Appleby to name but a few.

Newmarket has three major public horse exercise grounds: Warren Hill, Racecourse Side (situated between and alongside the Rowley Mile and July courses), and the Limekilns (including the Al Bahathri all-weather grounds). Godolphin also operate two large private horse exercise grounds near their Godolphin and Moulton Paddocks stables.

As there are two separate racecourses at Newmarket it features twice on the tour. Today is my 25th visit to the July course at Newmarket. Took the train from London to Newmarket via Cambridge and the courtesy coach to the racecourse.

I decided to oppose Dichato, the 7/4 favourite in the opening 6 furlong sprint, opting for Nicklaus instead. Nicklaus took a keen hold and was held up well in touch in the last pair, made an effort well over a furlong out, made no impression and was outpaced and weakened, finishing last of the six runners, 7 ¾ lengths behind Etefaaq. Dichato finished second, beaten by half a length.

I backed Theglasgowwarrior in the 2:40. He was held up in touch midfield, made headway to chase the leader a furlong out and stayed on but could make no impression on Mistress Quickly, the 100/30 favourite winner, who won by a comfortable 2 ½ lengths.

My selection in the third event was Hart Stopper, who was steadied at the start, raced in rear and made headway over a furlong out but could only finish second to Stanhope, the easy 10/1 winner, who was well in command in the final furlong and won comfortably by 3 lengths.

Another bout of seconditis awaited me in the 3:50 race. My choice, Raawy, took a keen hold, was held up in touch and looked promising just over 2 furlongs out. He went a clear second and kept on inside the final furlong but could make no impression on Saluti, the 9/4 winner, who beat him by 3 ½ lengths.

Khamaary, the 2/1 favourite carried the additional penalty of being my selection in the 4:25 race. She led, was ridden and hard pressed over a furlong out, was driven, headed, could find no extra and weakened towards the finish, finishing 2 lengths behind Makzeem the 4/1 winner, who led inside the final furlong and stayed on well.

I backed Surrey Hope, the 9/4 favourite in the 5:00. He raced centre and tracked the leaders and made an effort to press the leader 2 furlongs out but was unable to quicken and finished third, 3 ¼ lengths behind Rigoletto.

In the final event I chose Poet's Society, the 15/8 favourite. He led, was pushed along 2 furlongs out, was ridden and was hard pressed over a furlong out and headed inside the final furlong. He then battled back under pressure to lead again towards the finish, triumphing by a neck at the post.

I am off to Manchester for the weekend and going racing at York on Saturday before resuming my racecourse tour at Cartmel on Sunday.

Sunday 2nd July - Cartmel

Today is my seventh visit to Cartmel races but my first for eighteen years.

Cartmel village is located in Cumbria, 2 miles from Grange-over-Sands. It is known for its 12th Century Priory, and more recently as the "home of sticky toffee pudding", which can be purchased in various sizes from the Cartmel Village Shop. Cartmel is also noted for Simon Rogan's Michelin-star rated restaurant L'Enclume.

The racecourse is well hidden and is located behind the Post Office (honestly)!

Cartmel racecourse achieved notoriety in 1974 as it was the centre of the Gay Future attempted fraud by an Irish betting syndicate. The attempted fraud took place on the busiest day in the racing calendar with racing taking place on ten racecourse. Bets were made in numerous betting shops in London in doubles and trebles, which involved Gay Future in combination bets with two other horse trained by Scottish trainer Antony Collins in earlier races at other courses. On the day, these two additional horses were withdrawn shortly before the races; they were never intended to run and remained at their stables. Numerous bets therefore rolled over onto Gay Future as the conspirators had planned.

At his stables, Collins initially presented a poorly performing horse as if it were the real Gay Future. This raised the betting odds on offer, and the horse was entered in the Ulverston Novice Chase at Cartmel to be held on Bank Holiday Monday, 26th August 1974. The real horse was illicitly substituted for the imposter Arctic Chevalier in a lay-by on the M6.

Cartmel racecourse. A small isolated venue, had only one telephone line at the time connecting it to the outside world (there were no mobile phones back then!). This was deliberately kept engaged to prevent enquiries being made by betting firms headquarters, and the on course Tote was overworked by accomplices of the conspirators to prevent bets being placed on the horse, which would have lowered the odds from 10/1, Soap flakes were rubbed into the horse's legs to give the false impression that he was seating. Gay Future won easily, by 15 lengths, but bookmakers refused to pay out before an inquiry. In Ireland, however they paid out.

Following an investigation by Scotland Yard's Serious Crimes Squad, a trial was held at Preston Crown Court in February 1976. The two leading syndicate members were convicted of conspiracy to defraud the bookmakers. The trial judge fined Collins £1,00 combined with a suspended prison sentence. The UK's Jockey Club barred both men from British racecourses for ten years.

I took the train into Manchester today and on to Preston then on to Cark station, where a bus connection was waiting to take racegoers the 3 miles to Cartmel, I arrived in the village about 1:20pm and popped into a local hostelry for a pint of real ale, on what turned out to be quite a pleasant day.

The first race, a 2 mile 6 furlong hurdle, was at 2:20. I selected Oh So Gigolo, the 4/1 favourite, although I managed to secure nearly 13/2 on Betfair (7.4). Oh So Gigolo was deemed to be the 'best turned out' horse in the race, which is often the kiss of death (for some unknown reason) of a horse's prospects of winning the race. Oh So Gigolo made all was 4 lengths clear 3 out, a length ahead 2 out and pressed by the third on the run to the last. He was then ridden and held a narrow lead, was challenged by the 2nd on the run-in but held on well under pressure to score by a length. Pads fell at the first flight and spent most of the race running up and down the straight before being caught before the field turned for home.

The second race, a four runner event, was effectively a two horse race between Irish Roe the 8/13 favourite and The Wicket Chicken at 5/4. The other two runners started at 28/1 and 80/1. I decided to have a punt on The Wicket Chicken to upset the long odds-on favourite. She tracked the leader and led 3 out but was pushed along on the run to the last where she was challenged by Irish Roe, who was going ominously easily from a long way out, and ran on well under a hands and heels ride, winning by 1 ¾ lengths. The remaining two runners finished a further 63 and 23 lengths behind.

I selected Charlie Wingnut, one of the 3/1 joint favourites in the first steeplechase of the day at 3:20. He tracked the leaders, went 2nd at the 8th fence, led 4 out and drew clear and was seemingly presented with the race when Dursey Sound blundered at the 12th. Charlie WIngnut was 10 lengths clear at the last, was closed down by Presenting Junior, the other 3/1 joint favourite, on the long run-in. He responded gamely but just lost out in a sustained duel with the winner near the finish, going down by a head. The nearest challenger was a further 15 lengths behind.

As I wanted to get back to the Manchester area at a reasonable hour, I decided to make the 3:55 my last race of the day. The following train from Cark being over two hours later than the 16:39. My selection, Endeavor drifted badly in the market, was held up and was struggling from 4 out, eventually finishing last of the six runners, 39 lengths behind Domtaline, the 7/2 winner, who was all out to beat Red Riverman, an 8/1 chance, at the post.

56 courses down and only 5 to go now. Next stop on the racecourse tour, Haydock Park next Saturday.

Saturday 8th July - Haydock Park

Day 57 on the racecourse tour. Only 4 to go after today.

The current racecourse at Haydock Park was opened in 1899, although horse racing had been run in nearby Newton for many years, and the venue was used for hare-coursing in the 1880's. Haydock Park was awarded Racecourse of the Year in 1998 and 2000.

I took the 09:43 Virgin train from Euston to Wigan North Western today then a bus to Ashton-in-Makerfield followed by a 10-15 minute walk to the track.

Met my friend Robert on arrival at the racecourse then never saw him again all afternoon. A lovely sunny and warm day today with a big crowd to boot.

My selection in the opener was Humble Hero, the 11/4 favourite. He was slowly away and in rear before making some headway 3 furlongs out. After which he was driven 2 furlongs out and had every chance a furlong from home but was soon ridden and one pace thereafter. He finished fourth, 3 ¾ lengths behind Zenon, the 7/2 winner, who won going away.

I selected Abingdon, the favourite, in the second event, but I wanted at least 2/1 about it. However it went off the 6/4 favourite so I did not have a bet. This proved to be fortuitous, as she was beaten ½ a length into second place by The Black Princess, a 3/1 chance. Abingdon led 2 furlongs out, was ridden over a furlong out, ran on under pressure but was headed in the final 100 yards.

I backed both Kapstadt and Euchen Glen in the third race on the card, the Old Newton Cup. Kapstadt tracked the leaders, was in fourth half a mile from home before gradually losing place and finished seventh, 4 ¾ lengths behind Dylan Mouth, the 25/1 winner. Euchen Glen made an effort on the inner 3 furlongs out, did not have a clear run 2 furlongs out and had no chance thereafter but ran on in the final furlong, finishing ninth, 5 ½ lengths behind the winner.

I backed Pipers Note in the fourth race, a six furlong sprint. He ran creditably but could not get near either Magical Memory, the 13/8 winner or Kachy, the 11/8 favourite who was short-headed by the winner close home. Pipers Note finishing 4 lengths behind the runner up.

My selection in the 4:25 was Meshardal, an 11/1 chance. He was held up, made headway 2 furlongs out and led a furlong out but was soon ridden and headed in the final furlong, finishing third, 2 lengths behind Hart Stopper, the 4/1 winner.

I backed Roman Holiday in the 5:00, my last race of the day. He was held up, driven along over 2 furlongs out, was soon hard ridden and made no impression, finishing last of the eight runners, six lengths behind Excellent Sound, the 9/1 winner.

I missed the 5:30 race as I had a 6:30 train to catch from Wigan. However I did manage to find time in Wigan to pop into the Moon Under Water, a JD Wetherspoons pub for a pint and a curry before catching my train home.

Thursday 13th July - Doncaster

Well into the home straight now! Only three racecourses to go after today to complete my tour of all four corners of Great Britain.

From around the 16th century Doncaster embraced the wealthy stagecoach trade. This led to horse breeding in Doncaster, which in turn led to the start of horse races there. The earliest important race in Doncaster's history was the Doncaster Gold Cup, first run over Cantley Common in 1766. The Doncaster Cup is the oldest continuously regulated horse race in the world. A map of 1595 shows a racecourse at Town Moor. In 1600 the corporation tried to put an end to the races because of the number of ruffians they attracted, but in 1614 it acknowledged failure and instead marked out a racecourse.

Doncaster racecourse hosts the St Leger Stakes, the world's oldest classic horse race. During World War I the racecourse was used for military purposes and substitute races were run at Newmarket from 1915 to 1918.

I arrived at Doncaster Railway station around 1:20 pm and walked to the 1.7 miles to Doncaster Racecourse so arrived after the first race.

I decided to oppose James Garfield the 1/3 favourite in the second race, opting for Shuhood instead. James Garfield duly obliged at prohibitive odds. Shuhood finished last of the ten runners, 19 lengths behind the winner. I couldn't have got it more wrong if I had tried!

I didn't have a bet in the third race as I fancied King Of Paris, the favourite, but did not fancy his price of 10/11. I was considering having a small bet on the Eric Alston trained Maid In India. However I was put off by the fact that the yard had only had one winner from 37 runners this century. Needless to say Maid In India became their second at the rewarding odds of 33/1 (over double that on Betfair!). Maid In India stayed on well to lead close home. King Of Paris finished 6th, beaten by 7 ¼ lengths.

Similarly in the fourth race I fancied Tribute Act but not her price of Even Money. Tribute Act led close home to win by a head.

My selection in the fifth event was Powerful Dream, who was always towards the rear and finished seventh of the eight runners, beaten 9 ¼ lengths. Just Us Two won the race by a nose in a three way fight with You're Cool, the 3/1 favourite who just failed, and Archimedes who kept on well to finish third, only a head behind the runner-up.

I backed Kasperenko, the 9/4 favourite in the 4:25, but got 4/1 (5.0) on Betfair. He was held up towards the rear, made smooth headway 3 furlongs out, led on the bit a quarter of a mile from home, was shaken up inside the final furlong then went clear, winning by 2 ¾ lengths.

In the final race I backed Dusky Maid. She raced close up and disputed the lead two furlongs out before being ridden and driven approaching the final furlong and weakening to finish sixth of the seven runners, 5 ¾ lengths behind Arcadian Angel the 7/4 favourite who kept on well to get up in the dying strides and won by a short head from Totally Magic who was just held.

Wolverhampton and Uttoxeter next week then a short break before finishing off the tour at Salisbury on Monday 7th August.

Monday 17th July - Wolverhampton

I had intended to go racing at Wolverhampton last Thursday afternoon, however due to a major incident near Milton Keynes on the West Coast Main Railway Line all trains were cancelled from Euston until around lunchtime that day. I therefore rescheduled my trip to Wolverhampton for this evening on what was a lovely warm and sunny evening.

Today was my first visit to Wolverhampton races (aka Dunstall Park) for nearly 30 years and my first since it was converted to al All Weather track.

There has been a racecourse in Wolverhampton since 1825, in what is now the West Park, where the Park Road follows the line of the track. This was sold to the Corporation in 1878 and, after a gap of nine years, a new course was formed at Dunstall Park. In December 1993 the course was re-vamped with floodlights and a new all-weather Fibresand track alongside the turf track. In 2004 the Fibresand and turf tracks were replaced with a single Polytrack surface. In 2014, citing dissatisfaction with the degradation of the Polytrack surface, the course was closed for several months while a new artificial surface, Tapeta, was laid down.

I decided to drive to Wolverhampton today and only to stay for the first four races in order to get home at a reasonable hour.

I decided to oppose Amazing Alice, the 5/6 favourite in the opener, opting to back a first time out newcomer, Saxonroad Boy, trained by Richard Fahey and ridden by Tony Hamilton, the stable jockey. Saxonroad Boy started slowly and was outpaced throughout the 6 furlong contest, finishing eighth of the nine runners , ten lengths behind Amazing Alice, who made all and won easily by 2 ¼ lengths.

My selection in the 6:10 was Dyna Might. She raced prominently and led three furlongs out before being swallowed up and finishing fourth to Sheriff Garrett, finishing 6 ¼ lengths behind him.

I decided not to have a bet in the third race as my fancy Samarmadi did not represent sufficient value for me at 11/8 favourite. That proved to be a good decision as he was slowly into his stride and despite running on well could not quite get to Desert Rain who just held on by a short head.

In my last race of the evening I backed Never Say. She led until headed 10 furlongs out, chased the winner until ridden 2 furlongs out then weakened to finish last of the ten runners, beaten by 38 ½ lengths. Howardian Hill, a 33/1 outsider claimed the prize, winning by a length from the runner-up.

I had a great drive home, which only took around two hours.

Next stop Uttoxeter on Thursday, then various race meetings before rounding off the tour at Salisbury on Monday 7th August.

Wednesday 19th July - Uttoxeter

I am now fighting out the finish so to speak and approaching the winning post in racing parlance on my UK racecourse tour. Today is #60. Only Salisbury to go!

Uttoxeter's name has had at least 79 spellings since it was mentioned in the Domesday Book as "Wotochehede". Uttoxeter saw the last major royalist surrender of the English Civil War, on 25 August 1648, when James Hamilton, 1st Duke of Hamilton, surrendered to Parliamentarian General John Lambert.

Perhaps the most famous event to have occurred in Uttoxeter is the penance of Samuel Johnson. Johnson's father ran a bookstall in Uttoxeter market, and young Samuel once refused to help out on the stall. When Johnson was older, he stood in the rain (without a hat) as a penance for his failure to assist his father. This event is commemorated with the Johnson Memorial, which stands in Market Place in the town centre, and there is also an area of town called Johnson Road, which commemorates him.

In 1967 Champion jockey Josh Gifford equalled Fred Winter's record of 121 winners in a season at Uttoxeter on 15 June, the very last meeting of the 1966-67 National Hunt season. Half an hour later Gifford broke the record when he rode Red Flush to a ten lengths victory. In 1967 Rag Trade, owned by the flamboyant hairdresser Raymond 'Teasy Weasy' Bessone, won the Marston's Pedigree Midlands Grand National and followed-up by winning the Grand National at Aintree a few weeks later.

Today is my fifth visit to Uttoxeter races and my first in seven years.

My train arrived at Uttoxeter railway station, which is located adjacent to the racecourse, on schedule at 13:57. The first race, which had a schedule off time of 13:55 was in progress and the Malton Rose, the 8/13 hot favourite was winning with a ton in hand as I arrived at the course.

In the Premier Enclosure I asked a gentleman called Oliver to take my photograph and explained to him that I was visiting all the racecourse on the UK mainland this year. We stayed together for most of the rest of the afternoon and had a few bevvies together, exchanging racing stories including various racecourses we would like to visit on our respective bucket lists.

My first bet of the day was New Agenda in the 2:25. This five runner event basically boiled down to the top 3 in the market. New Agenda, the Even Money favourite, Lieutenant Gruber at 2/1 and Forgotten Hero at 9/2. New Agenda led until headed 3 out but was then driven and lost second before 2 out then soon lost touch with the leading pair. Lieutenant Gruber held a narrow lead at the last flight of hurdles, was hard ridden on the flat and ran on well, asserting in the final 100 yards to beat Forgotten Hero by 2 lengths, with New Agenda a remote third, a further 23 lengths behind.

My selection the third race, a 3 mile chase, was Free Of Charge, the 5/1 favourite. He was held up and made good progress to lead 4 out and was a length clear 3 out before being joined and headed 2 fences out and losing second place on the run-in, victory going to Classic Jewel a 10/1 chance. The winner stayed on well to triumph by 3 ¾ lengths from Solway Trigger, with Free Of Charge 2 lengths further adrift.

I decided to oppose Supreme Steel, the Evens favourite in the 3:35, opting for the Alan King trained Holy Street instead at 10/1. Holy Street raced in mid-division, was pushed along and made headway into 4th three out but was ridden, could find no extra and was beaten before 2 out. He finished fifth, 15 ½ lengths behind Supreme Steel, who found extra to win by 1 ¼ lengths when ridden and challenged by Lord Topper, a 12/1 shot on the run-in.

I backed two horses in the 4:10, Trafalgar Rock, which by chance is owned by a syndicate that my new found friend Oliver is involved with, and Cut The Corner. My unusual 'reason' for backing Cut The Corner, was that (in my opinion) he was led round by the best looking stable lass! Believe it or not I have actually managed to back a few good price winners (including one at 25/1) using this totally unscientific method! Trafalgar Rock was held up, was driven from 3 out and stayed on to finish third. Cut The Corner made headway to lead 2 out, was driven clear before the last and ran on well and was not extended, winning by a comfy 9 lengths.

As I am not a fan of 'bumpers' (National Hunt Flat races) I decided to make the 4:40 my last race of the day, my choice in which was Sweeping Rock. He was held up and made headway 3 out but was soon ridden and one paced, finishing 7th of the 11 runners, 42 ¾ lengths behind Stonecoldsoba, the 11/4 winner who was always going well and was in front and in command when making a slight mistake at the last before running-on well to win easily by 7 lengths from Vintage Salon, a 33/1 outsider.

So nearly there! Only Salisbury to go now in a couple of weeks' time.

Monday 7th August - Salisbury

Made it! 218 days after I started, my girlfriend Christine and I are at Salisbury races today to celebrate the end of my UK Mainland Racecourse Tour. Roughly 2 different racecourses a week.

Salisbury Cathedral, began in 1221 is considered a masterpiece of Early English architecture, and at 404 feet high, has the tallest spire in the UK. The site was supposedly established by shooting an arrow from Old Sarum, although this is certainly a legend as the distance is nearly 2 miles! The legend is sometimes amended to claim that the arrow struck a white deer, which continued to run and died on the spot where the cathedral is now sited. The spire's large clock was installed in 1386, and is one of the oldest surviving mechanical clocks in the world. The cathedral also contains the best-preserved of the four surviving copies of the Magna Carta.

Many great horses have won at Salisbury racecourse including Gimcrack (1768), Eclipse (1769), Sun Chariot (1941), Mill Reef (1970) and Sir Percy, winner of the 2006 Derby. Lester Piggott first rode in public at Salisbury in 1948 when he was an apprentice jockey aged twelve and weighing only five stone. It was here in 1949 that Winston Churchill first raced Colonist II in the one mile Upavon Stakes. The horse won, and went on to win the Ribblesdale Stakes at Royal Ascot later that year.

A 2 hour drive today, mostly on motorway, before driving through or near some more fantastically named rural villages such as Jacks Bush, Nether Wallop and Little Ann.

I popped in to Salisbury city for an hour before proceeding to the racecourse. I plan to return for a proper visit next year to do the place justice and go inside the historic cathedral.

An eight race card at Salisbury today. In the first race I opposed Ode To Autumn, the 8/11 favourite, opting for Ateem instead. Christine selected Ode To Autumn. I said I was not prepared to back it for her at the price but would give her Even money if it won. I did not have to pay up as Ode To Autumn could only manage a one-paced second, beaten a length by Move Over, the 12/1 winner. Ateem tracked the leaders but did not have the pace to challenge the winner, finishing fourth, beaten 4 lengths.

In the second event I selected Kitaabaat and Christine chose Bullingdon, the 9/4 favourite. Kitaabaat chased the leaders, was ridden to track the leading pair 2 furlongs out but could only manage did not have the pace to challenge. Bullingdon led inside the final furlong and kept on well to beat Magnificent by ½ a length. Kitaabaat finished 1 ¾ lengths behind the winner.

In the 3:00 both Christine and I backed Monteamiata, the 5/2 favourite. She raced in mid-division, was ridden 2 furlongs out and kept on in the final furlong but could not get on terms with Field Of Vision, the 9/2 winner, finishing 1 ¾ lengths behind him.

My main selection in the fourth race was Keeper's Choice. She was 7/1 in the morning paper and I thought I had got a good price of 12/1 (13.0) on Betfair. She opened at 16/1 on course and went off at 20/1! As it had drifted in the betting like the proverbial barge, I thought a small saver on another runner was advisable so I also backed Jazaalah, which was wearing the second colours of Sheikh Hamdan Al Maktoum. Awfaa, the 10/11 favourite. Christine backed Ambrosia, which started at 100/30. In a driving finish Keeper's Choice beat Ambrosia by a short head with Chalky a further short head behind in third.

In race 5 I backed Delirium and Christine backed Zaria. I claimed the minor bragging rights by my horse finishing 7 lengths in front of hers. Unfortunately Delirium was 6 ½ lengths and in seventh place behind Red Dragon, the 28/1 winner.

In the 4:30 I chose Captain Sedgwick and Christine selected Nightswift. Captain Sedgwick raced in mid-division, chased the winner over a furlong out but never threatened to get on terms. The winner, Love And Be Loved, was very keen on the way to the start, made all and stayed on well. Nightswift could only manage fifth, beaten 5 lengths.

In the penultimate event I chose So Sleek and Christine chose Harebell. So Sleek was held up, made headway over 2 furlongs out and ran on strongly to lead in the final 100 yards. Harebell did not have the pace to get on terms and faded to finish sixth.

In the last race we both selected Banff, which started the heavily backed 6/5 favourite, having opened on-course at 2/1. I had backed it on Betfair in the morning at just over 7/2 (4.66). However like all bar one of the favourites today he did not oblige and could only finish fourth to Ocean gale, the 9/1 easy winner, beaten 6 lengths.

2017 Racecourse Tour

Final Schedule

Day	Date	Racecourse	Day	Date	Racecourse	Day	Date	Racecourse
Mon	02 Jan	Plumpton	Sat	01 Apr	Stratford-On-Avon	Thu	11 May	Chester
Wed	04 Jan	Hereford	Sun	02 Apr	Ascot	Wed	17 May	York
Thu	05 Jan	Chelmsford City	Thu	06 Apr	Aintree	Sun	21 May	Market Rasen
Sat	07 Jan	Sandown Park	Fri	07 Apr	Sedgefield	Mon	22 May	Carlisle
Wed	18 Jan	Newbury	Sat	08 Apr	Chepstow	Tue	23 May	Brighton
Sat	21 Jan	Lingfield Park	Sun	09 Apr	Ffos Las	Wed	31 May	Beverley
Fri	10 Feb	Bangor-On-Dee	Mon	10 Apr	Kelso	Sat	03 Jun	Hexham
Sat	25 Feb	Kempton Park	Wed	12 Apr	Catterick Bridge	Mon	05 Jun	Thirsk
Sun	26 Feb	Fontwell Park	Fri	14 Mar	Bath	Wed	07 Jun	Hamilton Park
Tue	28 Feb	Leicester	Sat	15 Apr	Musselburgh	Tue	13 Jun	Yarmouth
Thu	02 Mar	Ludlow	Mon	17 Apr	Redcar	Wed	14 Jun	Worcester
Tue	07 Mar	Newcastle	Tue	18 Apr	Newmarket (Rowley)	Thu	22 Jun	Ripon
Thu	09 Mar	Wincanton	Thu	20 Apr	Cheltenham	Thu	29 Jun	Newmarket (July)
Tue	14 Mar	Southwell	Mon	24 Apr	Pontefract	Sun	02 Jul	Cartmel
Wed	15 Mar	Huntingdon	Wed	26 Apr	Epsom Downs	Sat	08 Jul	Haydock Park
Thu	16 Mar	Towcester	Thu	27 Apr	Perth	Thu	13 Jul	Doncaster
Fri	17 Mar	Fakenham	Mon	01 May	Windsor	Mon	17 Jul	Wolverhampton
Mon	20 Mar	Taunton	Tue	02 May	Nottingham	Wed	19 Jul	Utoxeter
Tue	21 Mar	Exeter	Sat	06 May	Goodwood	Mon	07 Aug	Salisbury
Wed	22 Mar	Warwick	Mon	08 May	Ayr			
Fri	31 Mar	Wetherby	Wed	10 May	Newton Abbot			

Plumpton	12:50	13:20	13:50	14:20	14:50	15:20	15:50	
02 Jan 2017	2m Hurdle	2m 1f Chase	2m 4f Hurdle	2m 4f Hurdle	3m 4f Chase	2m 4f Chase	2m Hurdle	
Selection	Sporty Yankee	Laissez Dire	No Comment	Ding Ding	Sartorial Elegance	Johns Luck	Shimba Hills	
SP	7/1	2/1	2/1	6/1	8/1	4/1	9/4 fav	
Fate	Finished 5th	Fell 9th	Won	Finished 3rd	Unseated 17th	Won	Won	
Hereford	12:55	13:25	13:55	14:25	14:55	15:25	15:55	
04 Jan 2017	3m 1f Hurdle	2m Hurdle	2m 5f Chase	2m Chase	2m 3f Hurdle	2m 3f Hurdle	2m Hurdle	
Selection	Late Shipment	Katy P	The Greenvet	Working Title	No Bet	Sandymount	Peruvien Bleu	
SP	5/1	14/1	66/1	15/8 fav	N/A	11/4	5/1	
Fate	Won	Finished 3rd	Unseated 9th	Fell 2nd	N/A	Finished 4th	Finished 15th	
Chelmsford City	17:45	18:15	18:45	19:15	19:45	18:15		
05 Jan 2017	1m AW Flat	2m AW Flat	5f AW Flat	5f AW Flat	1m 2f AW Flat	7f AW Flat		
Selection	Pendo	Western Prince	No bet	No Bet	Speedo Boy	Shypen		
SP	7/2 jf	100/30 jf	N/A	N/A	6/1	7/1		
Fate	Finished 3rd	Finished 5th	N/A	N/A	Won	Finished 8th		
Sandown Park	12:10	12:45	13:15	13:50	14:25	15:00	15:35	
07 Jan 2017	2m Hurdle	2m 4f Hurdle	2m 4f Chase	2m Chase	2m Hurdle	3m Chase	2m Hurdle	
Selection	No Bet	Lifeboat Mona	Atirelarigo	Garde La Victoire	No Bet	Rocky Creek	Robinshill	
SP	N/A	11/4 jf	5/1	6/4 fav	N/A	7/1	9/1	
Fate	N/A	Won	Fell 2nd	Won	N/A	Finished 11th	Finished 2nd	

Newbury	13:15	13:50	14:20	14:55	15:25	15:55		
18 Jan 2017	2m Hurdle	2m Hurdle	2m Chase	2m 7f Chase	2m 4f Hurdle	2m NH Flat		
Selection	No Bet	Royal Hall	Red Devil Star	Monbeg Gold	No Bet	Perfect Harmony		
SP	N/A	20/1	9/2	8/1	N/A	7/1		
Fate	N/A	Finished 5th	Unseated 7th	Finished 5th	N/A	Won		
Lingfield Park	12:50	13:25	14:00	14:35	15:10	15:45	16:15	
21 Jan 2017	1m AW Flat	1m AW Flat	1m 2f AW Flat	1m 4f AW Flat	1m 4f AW Flat	1m AW Flat	6f AW Flat	
Selection	Byres Road	No Bet	No Bet	Rock Steady	Green Or Black	Al Yarmouk	Bridge Builder	
SP	9/4	N/A	N/A	3/1	4/1	11/8 fav	9/2	
Fate	Finished 5th	N/A	N/A	Finished 2nd	Finished 5th	Finished 2nd	Won	
Bangor-on-Dee	13:50	14:20	14:50	15:20	15:55	16:25	17:00	
10 Feb 2017	2m 7f Hurdle	2m 4f Chase	2m Hurdle	3m 5f Chase	2m Hurdle	2m NH Flat	2m 4f Chase	
Selection	No Bet	Antartica De Thaix	Cosmos Des Obeaux	Themanfrom Minella	Surprise Vendor	Clondaw Rigger	No Bet	
SP	N/A	Evens fav	9/2	12/1	16/1	22/1	N/A	
Fate	N/A	Won	Finished 3rd	PU after 3 out	Finished 7th	Finished 5th	N/A	
Kempton Park	13:15	13:50	14:25	15:00	15:35	16:10	16:45	
25 Feb 2017	2m 5f Hurdle	2m Hurdle	2m 4f Chase	2m Hurdle	3m Chase	2m 4f Chase	2m NH Flat	
Selection	Coastal Tiep	No Bet	No Bet	Elgin	Double Shuffle	Sir Note	No Bet	
SP	11/2	N/A	N/A	3/1	11/2	07-Jan	N/A	
Fate	Finished 2nd	N/A	N/A	Finished 2nd	Finished 2nd	Won	N/A	

Fontwell Park	14:00	14:30	15:00	15:30	16:00	16:30	17:00	
26 Feb 2017	2m Chase	2m 5f Chase	2m 3f Hurdle	2m 3f Hurdle	3m 2f Chase	2m 6f Hurdle	2m 2f NH Flat	
Selection	Kilcrea Vale	King Of Glory	Different Gravey	Peak To Peak	Current Exchange	Ding Ding	No Bet	
SP	10/11 fav	4/1	2/1 jf	9/4	5/1	6/1	N/A	
Fate	Won	Finished 4th	Finished 5th	Finished 5th	Finished 2nd	Finished 5h	N/A	
Leicester	14:10	14:40	15:10	15:40	16:10	16:40		
28 Feb 2017	2m 4f Chase	2m 6f Chase	2m 6f Chase	2m 6f Chase	2m 4f Chase	2m 4f Chase		
Selection	Brice Canyon	No Bet	Rebel Rebellion	Powerful Symbol	Miss Oscarrose	Supreme Danehill		
SP	4/1	N/A	9/4 fav	15/8 fav	2/1 fav	2/1		
Fate	Finished 3rd	N/A	Finished 6th	Finished 2nd	Finished 2nd	Finished 3rd		
Ludlow	14:20	14:50	15:25	16:00	16:35	17:05	17:35	
02 Mar 2017	2m Hurdle	2m 4f Chase	2m 5f Hurdle	3m Chase	3m Hurdle	2m 4f Chase	2m Hurdle	
Selection	Coopers Square	Colin's Brother	Aliandy	Dusky Lark	No Bet	No Bet	No Bet	
SP	16/1	9/2	2/1 fav	8/1	N/A	N/A	N/A	
Fate	Pulled Up	Finished 3rd	Finished 4th	Finished 4th	N/A	N/A	N/A	
Newcastle	14:10	14:40	15:10	15:40	16:10	16:40		
07 Mar 2017	2m 4f Hurdle	2m 7f Chase	2m Hurdle	2m 4f Chase	2m Hurdle	2m NH Flat		
Selection	Broadway Belle	Plus Jamais	Manwell	Two Smokin Barrels	Midnight Moss	Sultans Pride		
SP	15/2	5/6 fav	3/1 jf	11/10 fav	4/1	11/4 jf		
Fate	Finished 3rd	Won	Finished 3rd	Won	Finished 2nd	Finished 3rd		

Wincanton	13:50	14:20	14:55	15:30	16:05	16:40	17:10	
09 Mar 2017	2m 3f Hurdle	2m Hurdle	3m 1f Chase	2m Hurdle	2m 3f Hurdle	3m 1f Chase	2m NH Flat	
Selection	Flow With Eve	Catchin Time	Flaming Charmer	No Bet	No Bet	Shanann Star	No Bet	
SP	7/1	5/1	7/2	N/A	N/A	8/1	N/A	
Fate	Finished 7th	Finished 3rd	Finished 3rd	N/A	N/A	Finished 2nd	N/A	
Southwell	13:10	13:45	14:25	15:05	15:45	16:25	17:00	
14 Mar 2017	1m 4f AW Flat	5f AW Flat	5f AW Flat	6f AW Flat	1m AW Flat	7f AW Flat	1m 4f AW Flat	
Selection	Storm King	Darvie	Borough Boy	Escalating	Dose	General Tufto	Go On Gal	
SP	2/1	4/1	11/4	2/1 fav	7/2	10/1	9/4 fav	
Fate	Finished 3rd	Finished 3rd	Finished 2nd	Finished 2nd	Finished 5th	Finished 2nd	Finished 2nd	
Huntingdon	13:45	14:25	15:05	15:45	16:25	17:05	17:40	
15 Mar 2017	2m Hurdle	2m 3f Chase	2m 4f Hurdle	1m 7f Hurdle	2m 7f Chase	3m 1f Hurdle	2m NH Flat	
Selection	Christmas In April	Miss Oscarrose	Meribel Millie	Quill Art	Celtic Tune	No Bet	No Bet	
SP	5/2	100/30 fav	7/4 fav	7/2 jf	4/1	N/A	N/A	
Fate	Finished 5th	Finished 4th	Finished 6th	Unseated Rider 3rd	Finished 2nd	N/A	N/A	
Towcester	13:20	13:55	14:35	15:15	15:55	16:35	17:15	
16 Mar 2017	2m 3f Hurdle	3m Chase	1m 7f Hurdle	2m 4f Hurdle	3m Chase	2m 7f Hurdle	3m Chase	
Selection	Daytime Ahead	General Girling	Celestial Magic	No Bet	No Bet	No Bet	No Bet	
SP	15/8 fav	9/2 jf	11/4	N/A	N/A	N/A	N/A	
Fate	Finished 6th	Won	Won	N/A	N/A	N/A	N/A	

Fakenham	14:00	14:40	15:20	16:00	16:40	17:15		
17 Mar 2017	2m Hurdle	3m Chase	2m Hurdle	2m Hurdle	3m Chase	2m 5f Chase		
Selection	Monfalcone	Little Windmill	Hint Of Grey	Whispering Storm	Rear Admiral	Tara Mac		
SP	16/1	7/1	11/4	3/1 fav	9/2	3/1 jf		
Fate	Finished 4th	Finished 4th	Won	Pulled Up Last	Finished 4th	Fell 12th		
Taunton	**14:20**	**14:50**	**15:20**	**15:50**	**16:20**	**16:50**		
20 Mar 2017	2m 3f Hurdle	2m Hurdle	2m 2f Chase	2m Hurdle	2m Chase	2m 7f Hurdle		
Selection	No Bet	No Bet	Mr Medic	Hint Of Mint	Knights Reward	No Bet		
SP	N/A	N/A	11/4 fav	11/4	9/2	N/A		
Fate	N/A	N/A	Unseated Rider 3 out	Fell 2nd last	Fell 4 out	N/A		
Exeter	**14:00**	**14:30**	**15:05**	**15:40**	**16:15**	**16:50**	**17:25**	
21 Mar 2017	2m Hurdle	2m 7f Hurdle	2m 2f Hurdle	2m 3f Chase	3m Chase	3m Chase	2m NH Flat	
Selection	Golan Dancer	Pure Vision	Martabot	No Bet	Kap Jazz	Kapgarde King	Just A Sting	
SP	5/2	100/30	9/1	N/A	7/4 fav	7/1	3/1	
Fate	Finished 2nd	Won	Finished 4th	N/A	Finished 3rd	Finished 4th	Won	
Warwick	**14:20**	**14:50**	**15:20**	**15:50**	**16:20**	**16:50**		
22 Mar 2017	2m 5f Hurdle	2m Hurdle	3m Chase	3m 2f Hurdle	sm 5f Hurdle	3m 5f Chase		
Selection	Oscars Boss	No Bet	Towering	Black Narcissus	Listen To The Man	Royals And Rebels		
SP	5/1	N/A	11/4	6/1	3/1	7/1		
Fate	Finished 5th	N/A	Finished 3rd	Finished 3rd	Finished 5th	Pulled Up 3 out		

Wetherby	14:20	14:50	15:20	15:50	16:20	16:50	17:20	
31 Mar 2017	2m Hurdle	2m Chase	2m 5f Hurdle	2m 5f Chase	2m Hurdle	3m Chase	2m NH Flat	
Selection	Master Of Finance	No Bet	Little Bruce	No Bet	Manwell	No Bet	No Bet	
SP	15/8	N/A	5/1	N/A	5/1	N/A	N/A	
Fate	Finished 2nd	N/A	Won	N/A	Finished 9th	N/A	N/A	

Stratford	13:40	14:10	14:45	15:20	15:55	16:30	17:05	17:35
01 Apr 2017	2m Hurdle	2m Hurdle	2m 2f Hurdle	2m 6f Chase	2m Hurdle	2m 6f Hurdle	2m 3f Chase	2m NH Flat
Selection	Don't Act Up	No Bet	Astrum	Pull The Chord	Star Foot	Viking Mistress	Guanciale	No Bet
SP	08-Jan	N/A	3/1	5/2 fav	11/4	10/1	12/1	N/A
Fate	Finished 7th	N/A	Won	Finished 2nd	Finished 2nd	Finished 6th	Finished 7th	N/A

Ascot	14:00	14:30	15:05	15:40	16:15	16:50	17:20	
02 Apr 2017	2m 3f Hurdle	2m Hurdle	2m 5f Chase	2m Chase	2m 7f Chase	2m 7f Hurdle	2m 5f Chase	
Selection	Tales Of The Tweed	Percy Street	Present Man	San Benedito	Masters Hill	Beneagles	No Bet	
SP	3/1 fav	7/2	15/8	11/4	11/2	7/2 jf	N/A	
Fate	Won	Finished 3rd	Won	Won	Finished 7th	Finished 5th	N/A	

Aintree	13:45	14:20	14:50	15:25	16:05	16:40	17:15	
06 Apr 2017	2m 3f Chase	2m 3f Hurdle	3m Chase	2m 4f Hurdle	2m 5f Chase	1m 7f Chase	1m 7f NH Flat	
Selection	Frodon	Divin Bere	Empire Of Dirt	The New One	Top Cat Henry	Theinval	No Bet	
SP	5/1	7/2	100/30	11/2	33/1	15/2	N/A	
Fate	Finished 5th	Finished 2nd	Pulled Up 3 out	Finished 3rd	Finished 16th	Finished 2nd	N/A	

Sedgefield	14:10	14:40	15:15	15:50	16:25	17:00	17:30	
07 Apr 2017	3m 2f Chase	2m Hurdle	2m 3f Hurdle	2m Hurdle	2m 5f Chase	3m 3f Hurdle	2m 3f Hurdle	
Selection	Cruisng Bye	Viserion	Stonebrigg Legend	Dark And Dangerous	Master Burbidge	Whatdoesthefoxsay	No Bet	
SP	14/1	7/4	13/2	9/2	11/8 fav	11/4	N/A	
Fate	Finished 8th	Finished 2nd	Finished 3rd	Pulled Up 2 out	Won	Finished 3rd	N/A	
Chepstow	13:40	14:15	14:50	15:30	16:05	16:40	17:35	18:05
08 Apr 2017	2m Hurdle	2m 3f Chase	2m 3f Hurdle	2m 7f Chase	2m Hurdle	2m 7f Chase	2m NH Flat	2m NH Flat
Selection	No Bet	Irish Thistle	Act Four	Petite Power	Thundering Home	Lac Sacre	No Bet	No Bet
SP	N/A	7/2 jf	12/1	11/4 jf	12/1	5/1	N/A	N/A
Fate	N/A	Finished 3rd	Won	Fell last	Finished 11th	Pulled up 14th	N/A	N/A
Ffos Las	14:15	14:45	15:20	15:55	16:30	17:00	17:30	
09 Apr 2017	2m 4f Hurdle	2m Chase	2m 3f Chase	2m 7f Chase	2m 7f Hurdle	2m 7f Chase	1m 7f NH Flat	
Selection	Ballyarthur	No Bet	Hansupfordetroit	Henllan Harri	Rocky's Treasure	Rocknrollrambo	No Bet	
SP	7/4	N/A	6/1	13/2	100/30 fav	13/8 fav	N/A	
Fate	Finished 2nd	N/A	Finished 4th	Finished 3rd	Won	Won	N/A	
Kelso	14:10	14:40	15:10	15:40	16:10	16:40	17:10	
10 Apr 2017	2m 6f Hurdle	2m 5f Chase	3m 2f Chase	2m 2f Hurdle	2m 1f Chase	3m 2f Chase	2m 2f Hurdle	
Selection	Buckled	Whitsundays	Ballyben	No Bet	Sky Full Of Stars	Five Piers	Surprise Vendor	
SP	4/1 fav	5/1	9/2	N/A	3/1	5/2 fav	11/1	
Fate	Finished 5th	Won	Finished 7th	N/A	Finished 4th	Finished 6th	Finished 75th	

Catterick	14:00	14:30	15:00	15:30	16:00	16:30	17:00	17:30
12 Apr 2017	5f Flat	1m 5f Flat	7f Flat	7f Flat	1m 3f Flat	6f Flat	6f Flat	5f Flat
Selection	Wishing Time	Surround Sound	Someone Exciting	Fingal's Cave	Be Perfect	Bold Spirit	Ambitious Icarus	Kinloch Pride
SP	4/1 jf	8/1	16/1	3/1	10/1	11/1	7/1	15/2
Fate	Won	Finished 4th	Finished 4th	Won	Won	Finished 7th	Finished 5th	Won

Bath	14:00	14:30	15:00	15:30	16:00	16:30	17:00	17:30
14 Apr 2017	5f Flat	5f Flat	1m 5f Flat	1m 3f Flat	5f Flat	1m Flat	5f Flat	5f Flat
Selection	No Bet	No Bet	No Bet	No Bet	No Bet	Invermere	Last Page	No Bet
SP	N/A	N/A	N/A	N/A	N/A	14/1	7/1	N/A
Fate	N/A	N/A	N/A	N/A	N/A	Finished 8th	Finished 2nd	N/A

Musselburgh	13:50	14:25	15:00	15:35	16:05	16:40	17:10
15 Apr 2017	7f Flat	5f Flat	1m Flat	1m 6f Flat	5f Flat	7f Flat	5f Flat
Selection	Roll On Rory	Monsieur Joe	Rashford's Double & Mailshot	Isharah	Requinto Dawn & Excellently Poised	War Of Succession	Royal Brave
SP	9/2 fav	5/2 jf	6/1 & 8/1	8/1	11/8 fav & 8/1	7/4 fav	4/1 fav
Fate	Finished 8th	Finished 5th	Finished 9th & 11th	Finished 7th	Finished 2nd & Won	Finished 3rd	Won

Redcar	14:05	14:35	15:10	15:45	16:20	16:55	17:30	18:00
17 Apr 2017	5f Flat	1m Flat	1m Flat	6f Flat	1m Flat	6f Flat	2m Flat	6f Flat
Selection	Kinloch Pride	Ninepin Bowler & Mellor Brook	Playwriter	Musharrif	Imperial Focus	No Bet	No Bet	No Bet
SP	6/1	11/2 & 6/1	7/1	12/1	8/1	N/A	N/A	N/A
Fate	Finished 2nd	Finished 4th & 3rd	Finished 3rd	Finished 9th	Finished 10th	N/A	N/A	N/A

Newmarket (Rowley Course)	13:50	14:20	14:55	15:30	16:05	16:35	17:05	
18 Apr 2017	1m Flat	5f Flat	7f Flat	1m Flat	1m 1f Flat	7f Flat	5f Flat	
Selection	Dawaaleeb	Sound And Silence & Frozen Angel	Mitigate	Repercussion	Khalidi	Mukalal	No Bet	
SP	10/1	7/2 fav & 18/1	25/1	20/1	7/2	7/1	N/A	
Fate	Finished 5th	Won & Finished 9th	Finished 6th	Finished 6th	Won	Finished 5th	N/A	
Cheltenham	14:05	14:40	15:15	15:50	16:20	16:55	17:30	
20 Apr 2017	2m 4f Hurdle	2m 4f Chase	2m 4f Hurdle	3m 2f Chase	2m 7f Hurdle	3m 1f Chase	2m NH Flat	
Selection	Brillaro Momento	No Bet	Carnspindle	Upswing	Mr Clarkson	Swincombe Scorchio	No Bet	
SP	9/1	N/A	15/2	4/1 fav	8/1	4/1	N/A	
Fate	Won	N/A	Finished 2nd	Won	Finished 7th	Finished 4th	N/A	
Pontefract	14:00	14:30	15:05	15:35	16:10	16:40	17:10	17:40
24 Apr 2017	5f Flat	1m Flat	5f Flat	2m 5f Flat	6f Flat	5f Flat	1m Flat	1m Flat
Selection	Sinaloa	Rockwood	Art Collection	La Fritillaire	Hitchcock & Noble Sword	Henley	Sakurajima	Reinstorm
SP	2/1 fav	5/1	10/1	5/2 fav	4/1 & 33/1	5/1	4/1	4/1
Fate	Finished 3rd	Finished 5th	Finished 6th	Finished 6th	Finished 5th & 6th	Finished 2nd	Finished 7th	Finished 5th
Epsom	14:10	14:45	15:15	15:50	16:25	17:00		
27 Apr 2017	5f Flat	1m 2f Flat	1m 4f Flat	1m 2f Flat	1m Flat	1m Flat		
Selection	Majestic Hero	Cracksman	Galapiat	Innocent Touch	No Bet	Vantage Point		
SP	9/2	4/6 fav	11/10 fav	4/1 fav	N/A	7/2 fav		
Fate	Won	Won	Won	Finished 7th	N/A	Finished 5th		

Perth	14:00	14:35	15:05	15:35	16:10	16:45	17:20	
28 Apr 2017	2m Hurdle	2m Chase	2m Hurdle	2m Chase	2m 4f Chase	3m 2f Hurdle	2m 4f Hurdle	
Selection	No Bet	Valseur Du Granval	Mash Potato	Chain Of Beacons	Special Catch	Total Assets	No Bet	
SP	N/A	2/1 fav	9/2	3/1	10/1	5/1	N/A	
Fate	N/A	Finished 4th	Finished 5th	Finished 3rd	Finished 2nd	Finished 2nd	N/A	
Windsor	14:00	14:35	15:05	15:45	16:20	16:55	17:30	
01 May 2017	6f Flat	6f Flat	1m Flat	1m Flat	1m 2f Flat	1m 3f Flat	5f Flat	
Selection	Flowing Clarets	King Of Spin	Cool Team	Wind In My Sails	Cape Banjo	No Bet	Midnightly	
SP	20/1	7/1	5/2	4/1 fav	3/1 fav	N/A		
Fate	Finished 10th	Won	Finished 2nd	Finished 7th	Finished 4th	N/A		
Nottingham	14:10	14:40	15:10	15:45	16:20	16:50	17:25	
02 May 2017	5f Flat	1m Flat	1m Flat	1m Flat	1m 2f Flat	1m 6f Flat	5f Flat	
Selection	Aquadabra	Khitaamy	Scribner Creek	La Casa Tarifa	Midnight Vixen	Brigadoon	Carlton Frankie	
SP	5/2 fav	25/1	7/2	5/4 fav	5/1	7/1	5/4 fav	
Fate	Finished 3rd	Finished 3rd	Finished 4th	Finished 5th	Finished 10th	Finished 2nd	Won	
Goodwood	13:35	14:05	14:40	15:15	15:50	16:25	17:00	17:30
06 May 2017	1m 6f Flat	1m 4f Flat	7f Flat	5f Flat	1m Flat	7f Flat	1m 2f Flat	1m 2f Flat
Selection	Miss Tiger Lily	Dubka	Zwayyan	Stepper Point	Intimation	No Bet	Dominating	Arab Moon
SP	8/1	11/4 fav	7/2 fav	8/1	9/4 fav	N/A	7/2 fav	11/4 fav
Fate	Finished 12th	Finished 5th	Finished 11th	Finished 8th	Finished 2nd	N/A	Finished 6th	Finished 5th

Ayr	14:00	14:30	15:00	15:30	16:00	16:30	17:00	
08 May 2017	5f Flat	5f Flat	6f Flat	7f Flat	1m 5f Flat	1m Flat	1m Flat	
Selection	No Bet	No Bet	Our Place In Loule	Arnold	Hayward Field	No Bet	Kiwi Bay	
SP	N/A	N/A	6/1 fav	13/8 fav	12/1	N/A	8/1	
Fate	N/A	N/A	Finished 3rd	Finished 4th	Finished 6th	N/A	Finished 7th	
Newton Abbot	14:05	14:35	15:10	15:45	16:15	16:45	17:15	
10 May 2017	2m 5f Hurdle	3m 1f Chase	2m Hurdle	2m 4f Chase	2m 5f Hurdle	2m Chase	2m Hurdle	
Selection	Momella	Master Jake	No Bet	Fox Appeal	Dites Rien	No Bet	Muffins For Tea	
SP	5/1	11/4	N/A	5/2	7/2 fav	N/A	2/1 fav	
Fate	Won	Pulled up 13th	N/A	Finished 2nd	Finished 3rdd	N/A	Won	
Chester	13:50	14:25	15:00	15:35	16:05	16:35	17:05	
11 May 2017	1m 2f Flat	1m 2f Flat	7f Flat	1m 4f Flat	5f Flat	6f Flat	1m 2f Flat	
Selection	No Bet	Poet's Word	Mutawatheb	Tamleek	No Bet	Munro	No Bet	
SP	N/A	4/1	7/2 jf	11/4	N/A	11/1	N/A	
Fate	N/A	Finished 2nd	Won	Finished 4th	N/A	Finished 2nd	N/A	
York	14:20	14:55	15:30	16:05	16:35	17:05	17:35	
17 May 2017	1m 2f Flat	6f Flat	6f Flat	1m 2f Flat	7f Flat	5f Flat	1m 4f Flat	
Selection	Lovell	Muntadab	The Tin Man	Vintage Folly	Starlight Romance	Savalas	No Bet	
SP	6/1 fav	6/1 jf	5/1	12/1	9/1	15-Feb	N/A	
Fate	Finished 20th	Finished 2nd	Finished 5th	Finished 2nd	Finished 3rd	Finished 5th	N/A	

Market Rasen	13:50	14:20	14:55	15:30	16:00	16:30	17:00	
21 May 2017	2m ½f Hurdle	2m ½f Hurdle	3m Chase	2m 4 ½f Hurdle	2m 3f Chase	3m Chase	2m ½f NH Flat	
Selection	No Bet	Jupiter Custos	No Bet	Viserion	Yorkist	Ultimatum Du Roy	Brecon Hill	
SP	N/A	12/1	N/A	10/1	7/2	3/1	11/10 fav	
Fate	N/A	Finished 3rd	N/A	Pulled Up 2 out	Finished 3rd	Finished 3rd	Won	
Carlisle	14:20	14:50	15:20	15:50	16:20	16:55	17:25	18:00
22 May 2017	5f Flat	6f Flat	1m Flat	7f Flat	7f Flat	7f Flat	7f Flat	2m 1f Flat
Selection	Ventura Dragon	Mr Orange	Ravenhoe	Il Sicario	Four Wishes	No Bet	No Bet	No Bet
SP	5/4 fav	4/1	12/1	7/2 fav	5/1	N/A	N/A	N/A
Fate	Won	Finished 4th	Finished 8th	Finished 5th	Finished 4th	N/A	N/A	N/A
Brighton	14:20	14:50	15:20	15:50	16:20	16:55	17:20	17:50
23 May 2017	6f Flat	7f Flat	7f Flat	1m 2f Flat	1m 2f Flat	1m Flat	1m Flat	6f Flat
Selection	Fusion Central	Pass The Cristal	No Bet	Deep Challenger	Provoking	Sheer Intensity	Buzz Lightyere	Duke Of North
SP	12/1	7/1	N/A	4/1 jf	7/1	4/1	11/8 fav	9/4 fav
Fate	Finished 8th	Won	N/A	Finished 2nd	Finished 7th	Won	Finished 3rd	Finished 6th
Beverley	14:00	14:30	15:00	15:30	16:00	16:30	17:00	17:30
31 May 2017	5f Flat	5f Flat	5f Flat	7 ½f Flat	1m ½f Flat	1m 2f Flat	7f Flat	1m 4f Flat
Selection	Our Little Pony	The Armed Man	Dundunah	Wink Oliver	Palmerston	Monsieur Glory	No Bet	No Bet
SP	7/4 fav	100/30	11/4 jf	7/1	5/2 fav	9/4 fav	N/A	N/A
Fate	Won	Finished 2nd	Finished 2nd	Finished 7th	Won	Finished 4th	N/A	N/A

Hexham	13:30	14:05	14:40	15:15	15:50	16:45	17:20	
03 Jun 2017	2m Hurdle	2m Hurdle	3m Chase	2m Hurdle	2m 4f Chase	2m 4f Chase	2m Hurdle	2m 7f Hurdle
Selection	Back To Balloo	No Bet	Hattons Hill	Beyondtemptation	Miss Conway	No Bet	No Bet	No Bet
SP	7/4 fav	N/A	11/4 fav	3/1	7/2 fav	N/A	N/A	N/A
Fate	Finished 2nd	N/A	Won	Fell 5th	Finished 2nd	N/A	N/A	N/A
Thirsk	14:00	14:30	15:00	15:30	16:00	16:35	17:05	
05 Jun 2017	6f Flat	6f Flat	1m 4f Flat	6f Flat	1m Flat	6f Flat	1m Flat	1m 4f Flat
Selection	Mabo	No Bet	My Renaissance	Meshardal	Kenstone	Stubytuesday	White Rosa	No Bet
SP	3/1	N/A	9/2	7/2 jf	15/2	11/2	11/4	N/A
Fate	Finished 7th	N/A	Finished 6th	Won	Won	Finished 9th	Finished 2nd	N/A
Hamilton	14:10	14:40	15:10	15:40	16:10	16:40	17:15	
07 Jun 2017	6f Flat	6f Flat	1m 5f Flat	1m Flat	1m 1f Flat	6f Flat	5f Flat	
Selection	Lina's Star	Don Valentino	No Bet	No Bet	Gulf Of Poets	Royal Connoisseur	Roy's Legacy	
SP	2/1	11/8 fav	N/A	N/A	9/2	5/1	9/2	
Fate	Finished 4th	Finished 2nd	N/A	N/A	Won	Finished 5th	Finished 4th	
Yarmouth	14:15	14:45	15:15	15:45	16:15	16:45	17:15	
13 Jun 2017	6f Flat	1m 3 ½f Flat	1m 2f Flat	1m Flat	1m Flat	7f Flat	6f Flat	
Selection	No Bet	Falak & St Andrews	Favorite Girl	Moolazim	Ocean Temptress	African Trader & Tigersin	No Bet	
SP	N/A	3/1 & 11/1	7/2	9/2	11/4 fav	8/1 & 4/1 fav	N/A	
Fate	N/A	Finished 3rd & 4th	Finished 2nd	Won	Finished 2nd	Finished 6th & 8th	N/A	

Worcester	14:20	14:50	18:40	15:50	16:20	16:50	17:20	17:50
14 Jun 2017	2m 1/2f Chase	2m 7f Chase	2m NH Flat	2m 4f Hurdle	2m 4f Hurdle	2m 4f Hurdle	2m 7f Hurdle	2m 7f Hurdle
Selection	Desertmore Hill	Mahlers Star	Madam Anna	Lake Chapala	Three Star General	Deebaj	No Bet	No Bet
SP	2/1 fav	7/1	8/1	7/2	13/8	3/1	N/A	N/A
Fate	Won	Finished 5th	Finisahed 5th	Finished 4th	Won	Finished 2nd	N/A	N/A

Ripon	14:10	14:45	15:20	15:55	16:35	17:10	17:45
22 Jun 2017	6f Flat	6f Flat	5f Flat	1m 4f Flat	1m 1f Flat	1m 4f Flat	1m Flat
Selection	Noah Amor	Collingham Park	Oriental Splendour	Phoenix Dawn	Sands Chorus	Presenting Julio	No Bet
SP	10/1	7/1	5/2 fav	11/2	5/2 fav	7/4 fav	N/A
Fate	Finished 5th	Finished 2nd	Finished 6th	Finished 3rd	Finished 4th	Finished 10th	N/A

Newmarket (July Course)	14:10	14:40	15:15	15:50	16:25	17:00	17:35
29 Jun 2017	6f Flat	1m 4f Flat	6f Flat	7f Flat	7f Flat	1m Flat	5f Flat
Selection	Nicklaus	Theglasgowwarrior	Hart Stopper	Raawy	Khamaary	Surrey Hope	Poet's Society
SP	100/30	9/2	11/4	4/1	2/1 fav	9/4 fav	15/8 fav
Fate	Finished 6th	Finished 2nd	Finished 2nd	Finished 2nd	Finished 5th	Finished 3rd	Won

Cartmel	14:20	14:50	15:20	15:55	16:25	17:00	17:35
02 Jul 2017	2m 6f Hurdle	2m 1f Hurdle	3m 1 ½f Chase	2m 1f Chase	2m 5f Chase	3m 1f Hurdle	2m 1f Hurdle
Selection	Oh So Gigolo	The Wicket Chicken	Charlie Wingnut	Endeavor	No Bet	No Bet	No Bet
SP	4/1 fav	5/4	3/1 jf	11/4	N/A	N/A	N/A
Fate	Won	Finished 2nd	Finished 2nd	Finished 6th	N/A	N/A	N/A

Haydock Park	14:05	14:40	15:15	15:50	16:25	17:00	17:30	
08 Jul 2017	1m 6f Flat	1m 4f Flat	1m 4f Flat	6f Flat	6f Flat	7f Flat	1m 2 ½f Flat	
Selection	Humble Hero	No Bet	Kapstadt & Euchan Glen	Pipers Note	Meshardal	Roman Holiday	No Bet	
SP	11/4 fav	N/A	9/1 & 18/1	5/1	11/1	4/1	N/A	
Fate	Finished 4th	N/A	Finished 7th & 9th	Finished 3rd	Finished 3rd	Finished 8th	N/A	
Doncaster	13:40	14:10	14:45	15:20	15:55	16:25	16:55	
13 Jul 2017	2m ½f Flat	6f Flat	6f Flat	1m Flat	5f Flat	1m 4f Flat	7f Flat	
Selection	No Bet	Shuhood	No Bet	No Bet	Powerful Dream	Kasperenko	Dusky Maid	
SP	N/A	7/1	N/A	N/A	5/1	9/4	5/1	
Fate	N/A	Finished 10th	N/A	N/A	Finished 7th	Won	Finished 6th	
Wolverhampton	17:40	18:10	18:40	19:10	19:40	20:10	20:40	
17 Jul 2017	6f AW Flat	1m 6f AW Flat	6f AW Flat	1m 4f AW Flat	1m 1 ½f AW Flat	1m ½f AW Flat	7f AW Flat	
Selection	Saxonroad Boy	Dyna Might	No Bet	Never Say	No Bet	No Bet	No Bet	
SP	16/1	12/1	N/A	11/1	N/A	N/A	N/A	
Fate	Finished 8th	Finished 4th	N/A	Finished 10th	N/A	N/A	N/A	
Uttoxeter	13:55	14:25	15:00	15:35	16:10	16:40	17:15	
19 Jul 2017	2m 4f Hurdle	2m Hurdle	3m Chase	2m 7f Hurdle	2m 4f Chase	2m Hurdle	2m NH Flat	
Selection	No Bet	New Agenda	Free Of Charge	Holy Street	Trafalgar Rock & Cut The Corner	Sweeping Rock	No Bet	
SP	N/A	Evens fav	5/1 fav	10/1	9/4 fav & 11/2	7/2	N/A	
Fate	N/A	Finished 3rd	Finished 3rd	Finished 5th	Finished 3rd & Won	Finished 7th	N/A	

Salisbury	14:00	14:30	15:00	15:30	16:00	16:30	17:00	17:35
07 Aug 2017	7f Flat	7f Flat	6f Flat	1m Flat	1m Flat	1m Flat	1m 4f Flat	1m 6f Flat
Selection	Ateem	Kitaabaat	Monteamiata	Keeper's Choice & Jazaalah	Delirium	Captain Sedgwick	So Sleek	Banff
SP	7/1	4/1	5/2 fav	20/1 & 20/1	11/2	11/4 fav	4/1	6/5 fav
Fate	Finished 4th	Finished 4th	Finished 4th	Won & Finished 9th	Finished 7th	Finished 2nd	Won	Finished 4th

#1 Plumpton 2nd January

_**#2 Hereford 4th January**

#3 Chelmsford City 5th January

#4 Sandown Park 7th January

#5 Newbury 18th January

#6 Lingfield Park 21st January

#7 Bangor-on-Dee 10th February

#8 Kempton Park 25th February

#9 Fontwell Park 26th February

#10 Leicester 28th February

#11 Ludlow 2nd March

#12 Newcastle 7th March

#13 Wincanton 9th March

#14 Southwell 14th March

#15 Huntingdon 15th March

#16 Towcester 16th March

#17 Fakenham 17th March

#18 Taunton 20th March

#19 Exeter 21st March

#20 Warwick 22nd March

#21 Wetherby 31st March

#22 Stratford-upon-Avon 1st April

#23 Ascot 2nd April

#24 Aintree 6th April

#25 Sedgefield 7ᵗʰ April

#26 Chepstow 8ᵗʰ April

#27 Ffos Las 9th April

#28 Kelso 10th April

#29 Catterick 12ᵗʰ April

#30 Bath 14ᵗʰ April

#31 Musselburgh 15th April

#32 Redcar 17th April

#33 Newmarket (Rowley Course) 18th April

#34 Cheltenham 20th April

#35 Pontefract 24th April

#36 Epsom 26th April

#37 Perth 27th April

#38 Windsor 1st May

#39 Nottingham 2nd May

#40 Goodwood 6th May

#41 Ayr 8ᵗʰ May

#42 Newton Abbot 10ᵗʰ May

#43 Chester 11th May

#44 York 17th May

#45 Market Rasen 21st May

#46 Carlisle 22nd May

#47 Brighton 23rd May

#48 Beverley 31st May

#49 Hexham 3rd June

#50 Thirsk 5th June

#51 Hamilton Park 7ᵗʰ June

#52 Yarmouth 13ᵗʰ June

#53 Worcester 14th June

#54 Ripon 22nd June

#55 Newmarket (July Course) 29th June

#56 Cartmel 2nd July

#57 Haydock 8th July

#58 Doncaster 13th July

#59 Wolverhampton 17th July

#60 Uttoxeter 19th July

#61 Salisbury 7th August

A few more photos taken along the way !

22nd March Warwick

My friend Graham Clark with Absolutely Frankie (a horse he owns a share of, and with jockey Zak Baker)

6th May Goodwood

10th May Newton Abbot

11th May Chester

21st May Market Rasen

14th June Worcester (with my good friend Maurice)

Printed in Great Britain
by Amazon